Conrad and Cinema

Ars Interpretandi
The Art of Interpretation

Raymond Gay-Crosier
General Editor

Vol. 4

PETER LANG
New York • Washington, D.C./Baltimore • San Francisco
Bern • Frankfurt am Main • Berlin • Vienna • Paris

Gene D. Phillips

Conrad and Cinema

The Art of Adaptation

PETER LANG
New York • Washington, D.C./Baltimore • San Francisco
Bern • Frankfurt am Main • Berlin • Vienna • Paris

PR
6005
·O4
Z78496
1995

Library of Congress Cataloging-in-Publication Data

Phillips, Gene D.
  Conrad and cinema : the art of adaptation/ Gene D. Phillips.
      p. cm. — (Ars interpretandi; vol. 4)
  Includes bibliographical references.
    1. Conrad, Joseph, 1857-1924—Film and video adaptations. 2. English
fiction—Film and video adaptations. 3. Motion pictures and literature.
I. Title. II. Series: Ars interpretandi (New York, N.Y.); v. 4.
  PR6005.04Z78496   823'.912—dc20   94-30263
  ISBN 0-8204-2669-5
  ISSN 1043-5778

Die Deutsche Bibliothek-CIP-Einheitsaufnahme

Phillips, Gene D.:
Conrad and cinema : the art of adaptation/ Gene D. Phillips. - New York;
Washington, D.C./Baltimore; San Francisco; Bern; Frankfurt am Main;
Berlin; Vienna; Paris : Lang.
  (Ars interpretandi; Vol. 4)
  ISBN 0-8204-2669-5
NE: GT

The paper in this book meets the guidelines for permanence and durability
of the Committee on Production Guidelines for Book Longevity of the
Council of Library Resources.

© 1995 Peter Lang Publishing, Inc., New York

Printed in the United States of America.

To
Fred Zinnemann
Another artist in exile

Contents

Foreword:
Filmmaker versus Fiction Writer

Graham Greene

I have long suspected that a high-class murder is the simple artistic ideal of most film directors.

—Graham Greene

I have sometimes doubted Alfred Hitchcock's talent. As a director he has always known the right place to put his camera (and there is only one right place in any scene), he has been pleasantly inventive with his sound; but as a producer and as a writer of his own scripts he has been appallingly careless: he has cared more for an ingenious melodramatic situation than for the construction and continuity of his story. In *Sabotage*, which is derived from Conrad's *Secret Agent*, for the first time he has really "come off."

Sabotage is not, of course, Conrad's *Secret Agent*. That dark drab passionate tale of Edwardian London could never find a place in the popular cinema, and only Jacques Feyder, I think the director of the silent version of Zola's *Thérèse Raquin*, could transfer its peculiar qualities—of madness and despair in four-wheelers and backstreets—to the screen. But Mr. Hitchcock's adaptation of Conrad's novel is on a different level from his deplorable adaptation of Somerset Maugham's *Ashenden* stories: his version of Conrad's melodrama is convincingly realistic, perhaps because Hitchcock has left the screenplay to other hands.

The story retains some of the ruthlessness of the original. Mr. Verloc is no longer an *agent provocateur*, but a straightforward destructive agent of a foreign power, who keeps a tiny independent cinema in the East End, and the film opens with his secret return home one night during a sudden blackout. (Hitchcock has not overcome in these sequences the difficulty of lighting a blackout—how far a little candle throws its beams!)

Mr. Verloc has succeeded in causing the blackout by getting sand into the Battersea generators, but his employers are not satisfied with his anarchistic activities. He is told to disrupt the parade on Lord Mayor's day by laying a bomb in the cloakroom at Piccadilly Circus. . . .

He is closely watched by the police, and he has to entrust the bomb to his wife's small brother Stevie, who, delayed by the procession, is blown to fragments with a busload of people. Mrs. Verloc, after hearing the news, passes through the little cinema hall to her living room. A children's matinée is in progress, and Walt Disney's *Cock Robin* is on the screen. She is pursued by the children's laughter and the repetitions of the song, "Who Killed Cock Robin?" This ingenious and pathetic twist is stamped as Hitchcock's own; but unlike so many of his ideas in the past, it is an integral part of the story (it is linked to Stevie's death); and it leads on to the admirably directed scene when Mrs. Verloc, serving dinner to her husband, finds herself against her own will continually picking up the carving knife—to serve the potatoes, to scoop up the cabbage, to kill Mr. Verloc.

A happy ending, of course, has to be contrived: Mr. Verloc's body is plausibly disposed of; a young detective is there to marry her—but this is all managed with a minimum of offense. Mr. Hitchcock has been helped by admirable dialogue, written by Ian Hay and Helen Simpson, and a fine cast, a cast with only two weak members: Mr. John Loder as the detective is unconvincing; and for Desmond Tester's prep school accent as Stevie I feel an invincible distaste. Oscar Homolka, a slow, kindly, desperate Mr. Verloc, and Sylvia Sidney as his innocent wife raise the melodrama at times to the tragic level; and William Dewhurst gives a superb performance as the Professor, a soapy old scoundrel who supports his shrewish daughter and her bastard child with a bird business, concocting his explosives in the one living room among the child's dolls and the mother's washing.

This is popular cinema at its best. The cinema, after all, must appeal to the millions (as this film does). We have to accept its popularity as a virtue, not turn away from it as a vice. The novelist may write for a few thousand readers, but the film artist must work for the millions.

Acknowledgments

First of all, I am most grateful to Sir Alfred Hitchcock, Sir Carol Reed, Richard Brooks, and Francis Coppola, all of whom have made Conrad films, and who were willing to talk with me in the course of the long period in which I was engaged in remote preparation for this study.

Graham Greene's essay on film versus fiction, which appears as the Foreword of this book, is reprinted with the kind permission of the author from *Graham Greene: Collected Film Criticism*, edited by John Russell Taylor (New York: Simon and Schuster, 1972), pp. 122-23.

I would also like to single out the following people among all those who have assisted me:

Charles Silver of the Museum of Modern Art Film Study Center in New York, and the staff of the Motion Picture Section of the Library of Congress in Washington, for the use of their research facilities.

Research materials were also obtained from the Orson Welles file of the RKO Collection at the University of Los Angeles; and the Henry W. and Albert A. Berg Collection of the New York Public Library, Astor, Lenox, and Tilden Foundations for Conrad's letters to his agent, J. B. Pinker.

A Conrad Chronology

1857   Jozef Teodor Konrad Korzeniowski, born in the Polish Ukraine, December 3, to Apollo Korzeniowski and Ewa Brobowska. (He later took Joseph Conrad as his pen name.)

1862   Apollo and Ewa Korzeniowski are banished to northern Russia for advocating the violent overthrow of the Russian regime in Poland. Their son Joseph accompanies them.

1878   Despondent over his mounting debts, he attempts suicide in February by shooting himself in the chest, an act which presages the suicides dramatized in his fiction; e.g., *Victory* and *The Secret Agent.* Joins his first British ship as an ordinary seaman.

1886   Becomes a British subject. Passes his examination as Master Mariner of the British Merchant Marine, which entitles him to command seagoing vessels.

1890   Works in the Belgian Congo. His experiences are recalled in *Heart of Darkness.*

1894   Leaves his last position as a British seaman.

1895   *Almayer's Folly,* his first novel, published.

1896   *Outcast of the Islands,* his second novel, published. Marries Jessie George.

1897   *The Nigger of the Narcissus* published.

1900   *Lord Jim* is published.

1902   *Youth and Two Other Tales* published.

1903   *Romance,* a novel written in collaboration with Ford Madox Ford, published.

1904   *Nostromo* published.

1907   *The Secret Agent* published.

1911   *Under Western Eyes* published.

1913   *Chance* published.

1915   *Victory* published.

1917   *The Shadow Line* published.

1919   Receives nearly £4,000 for the American screen rights to his fiction. *The Arrow of Gold* published. Release of the first film version of *Victory.*

1920   *The Rescue* published. Composes his only film scenario,
       The Strong Man, based on "Gaspar Ruiz."
1922   His dramatization of *The Secret Agent* produced in
       London.
1923   *The Rover* published.
1924   Dies of a heart attack on August 3.
       Buried in Canterbury near his home.
1925   Release of the first film version of
       Lord Jim.
1926   Release of *The Silver Treasure,* the film version of
       Nostromo.
1927   Release of *The Road to Romance,* film version of *Romance.*
1929   Release of the film version of *The Rescue.*
1930   Release of *Dangerous Paradise,* the second film version of
       Victory.
1936   Release of *Razumov,* film version of *Under Western Eyes.*
       Release of *Sabotage,* film version of *The Secret Agent.*
1940   Release of *Victory,* the third film version of *Victory.*
1952   Release of the film version of *An Outcast of the Islands.*
1952   *Face to Face* (an omnibus film which includes a film
       version of "The Secret Sharer") released.
1954   Release of *Laughing Anne,* the film version of "Because
       of the Dollars."
1965   Release of the second film version of *Lord Jim.*
1967   Release of the film version of *The Rover.*
1973   Release of the second film version of "The Secret
       Sharer."
1977   Release of *The Duellists,* the film version of *The Duel.*
1979   Release of *Apocalypse Now,* film version of *Heart of
       Darkness.* Release of *The Heart of the Forest,* another
       film version of *Heart of Darkness.*
1994   Premiere of *Heart of Darkness,* made-for-cable version of
       the novella.

List of Illustrations

1. Alfred Hitchcock directing Oscar Homolka in *Sabotage*, based on Joseph Conrad's *The Secret Agent*. (Museum of Modern Art/Still Film Archive)

2. Ramon Novarro in The *Road to Romance*, based on the novel *Romance* by Joseph Conrad and Ford Maddox Ford. (Museum of Modern Art/Still Film Archive)

3. Ronald Colman and Lily Damita in *The Rescue*. Ronald Colman plays Captain Tom Lingard, the same role played by Ralph Richardson in *An Outcast of the Islands* twenty-two years later. (Museum of Modern Art/Film Stills Archive)

4. Jack Holt confronts Bull Montana, Lon Chaney, and Ben Deely in the first version of *Victory*. (Museum of Modern Art/Film Stills Archive)

5. Gustav von Seyffertitz (left) and Francis McDonald (right) menace Warner Oland (middle) in the second version of *Victory*, called *Dangerous Paradise*. (Museum of Modern Art/Film Stills Archive)

6. Fredric March is suspicious about Sig Rumann in the third version of *Victory*. (Museum of Modern Art/Film Stills Archive)

7. Michel Simon, the distinguished French actor in *Razumov*, the French film of *Under Western Eyes*. (Museum of Modern Art/Film Stills Archive.

8. Sylvia Sidney and Desmond Tester examine a sailboat as the villain of *Sabotage*, based on Conrad's *Secret Agent*, eyes

Introduction: Paint versus Plaster

You can't say the same thing with a moving picture as you can with a book, any more than you can express with paint what you can with plaster.

—William Faulkner

I am not averse to taking all the shekels I can garner from the movies. Because you can always say, "Oh, but they put on the movie in a different spirit from the way it was written!"

—F. Scott Fitzgerald

The distinguished film maker Josef Von Sternberg once remarked that fiction and film have both fed at the same breast. This is a rather picturesque way of observing how often film studios have turned to the novels of writers like Conrad for material, given the affinities between fiction and film. This simple observation, then, has articulated for me in simple terms the basic thrust of this book, which is an examination of the relationship of fiction and film, as reflected in the screen versions of the works of one novelist: Joseph Conrad.

As Joy Boyum notes in her book on film versions of fiction, Hollywood from the very dawn of cinema history turned to works of fiction as source material for films. In fact, during the silent period D. W. Griffith, often called the Father of Motion Pictures, derived some of his films from fictional works; e.g., he made short film versions of Jack London's *Call of the Wild* (1908) and Charles Dickens's *Cricket on the Hearth* (1909). In addition, he turned Thomas Burke's story, "The Chink and the Child," into one of his most popular feature films, *Broken Blossoms* (1919). Indeed, as early as 1911, critic Stephen Bush wrote in *The Moving Picture World* that literary classics invite filming, since a work that has pleased many generations "is most likely to stand the test of cinematographic reproduction."

Commenting on Bush's statement, Boyum remarks, "Literature attracted film makers back then for the same reason it does today. On the most practical levels, it supplied motion pic-

tures with a much-needed source of plot and characters." And if
the work in question also happened to be a popular novel, "it
also made for that most valuable of screen assets: the proverbial
'proven property.'" Nevertheless, even in the hands of a Griffith, Boyum goes on to say, silent pictures "remained significantly limited as a storytelling medium," precisely because of
the absence of spoken dialogue: "For its narrative and dramatic
possibilities to be in any way fulfilled, film clearly demanded
sound."[1]

With the advent of sound in the late Twenties, then, the
movies learned to talk; and the motion picture industry turned
more than ever to fictional works for new properties to film.
Looking back on the birth of the sound era in his essay on film
production in the *Encyclopedia Britannica,* Alfred Hitchcock
wrote that the introduction of spoken dialogue constituted the
final touch of realism needed by the film medium.

But that, of course, did not mean that film makers should
abandon the mobility of the camera and other cinematic techniques that had been perfected in the silent era, thereby forget-
ting that talking pictures should still be moving pictures. In
"pure cinema," Hitchcock continued, "dialogue would always be
designed as a complement to the visual images; and a good
director would never rely too heavily on the spoken word."
Hitchcock accordingly insisted that a good adaptation of a literary work to the screen involved creating a film in which the
images as often as possible were allowed to speak for themselves. After all, one of the most basic elements of the cinema is
the telling of a story as visually as possible, Hitchcock went on:
"to embody the action in the juxtaposition of images that have
their own specific language and emotional impact—that is cinema."[2]

As the sound era progressed, Hollywood turned out an end-
less number of impressive films derived from works of fiction,
which Hitchcock would have endorsed as "pure cinema": from
Emily Brontë's *Wuthering Heights* (1939), Hemingway's *To Have
and Have Not* (1944), Dickens's *Great Expectations* (1946), and
Greene's *Our Man in Havana* (1959), to Hardy's *Far from the
Madding Crowd* (1967), Lawrence's *Women in Love* (1969),
Fitzgerald's *The Great Gatsby* (1974), Forster's *A Passage to India*

(1984), and Wharton's *The Age of Innocence* (1993). And there is, of course, no end in sight.

The present volume is meant to be a companion piece to the present author's previous studies of the film adaptation of the fiction of other great writers. Indeed, the primary purpose of this study is to determine to what extent the films of Conrad's fiction—all of which were scripted by other hands—are worthy renditions of the stories from which they were derived.

Much has been written on the theoretical level about the relationship of film and fiction, ranging from George Bluestone's groundbreaking *Novels into Film* to Joy Gould Boyum's *Double Exposure: Fiction into Film*. The purpose of my present study is to show how the wedding of fiction and film works out concretely in an analysis that is based on literary and cinematic theory about the nature of the two media, but which focuses on the screen versions of the fiction of a single novelist.

Later in these introductory remarks, therefore, I shall briefly analyze the nature of fiction and film as two separate media, in order to show how they are different and how they are similar. The succeeding chapters will then examine the motion pictures based on Conrad's work in the context of the critical theory developed at the beginning of the book. In taking up each of Conrad's works that has been filmed, I shall first consider it as a literary work in its own right, independent of the fact that it was later filmed; for it is only by understanding the significance of each story as Conrad conceived it that we can judge the relative artistic merits of the subsequent screen version, and consequently come to a firmer grasp of the relationship of fiction to film. Let us spend a little time, therefore, in sketching the relationship of film and fiction, so that we can better appreciate the films made from Conrad's work in the chapters to come.

First of all, let me point out that, in general, cinema has more in common with fiction than with any other form of literature. One might be tempted to suppose that film is closer to drama than to fiction, since a play—like a motion picture—is acted out before an audience. But the similarity really ends there. Both a novel and a film depend more on description and narration than on dialogue, while in a play the emphasis is reversed.

Film historian Rick Altman reminds us that an article by the Russian film director Sergei Eisenstein *(Potemkin),* entitled "Dickens, Griffith, and the Film Today," "now serves as the *locus classicus* of an important strain of criticism stressing direct ties between film and the novel. . . . What is consistently remembered from Eisenstein's juxtaposition of the British novelist and the American film maker is a clear statement of influence: Griffith learned important aspects of his craft by paying close attention to the technique of Dickens." Dickens is invoked by Eisenstein, Altman continues, "because of his use of episodic structures, his tendency toward overstated, oversimplified emotions, and his contributions to the technique of crosscutting."

Altman concludes, "What Eisenstein claimed in a limited context, others have raised to the level of general pronouncement: a fundamental continuity connects the narrative technique" of the novel and the dominant style of motion pictures.[3] Thus Robert Nathan, in affirming that film is closer to fiction than to drama, calls a movie a novel to be seen instead of read. This is because a motion picture, like a novel, "ranges where it pleases; i.e., it deals in description and mood; it follows, by means of the camera, the single, unique vision of the writer." On the other hand, "you will find in every novel the counterparts of long shots and close-ups, trucking shots, and dissolves; but you will find them in words addressed to the ear, instead of pictures meant for the eye."[4]

Fiction versus Film

Nevertheless, in emphasizing the close relationship that undoubtedly exists between fiction and film, one must not forget that they still remain two different media of expression. For one thing, a film, as a product of the commercial cinema, must appeal to a mass audience, as Graham Greene indicates in his Foreword to this book, in order to make a profit. Thus a novel can sell 20,000 copies and still show a profit, while a film, by contrast, must reach millions to be profitable.

On the other hand, Greene never felt that box office popularity should be the sole index of a film's worth. "Does reaching the public necessarily mean reaching the biggest, most amorphous public possible?" he asked in an article in the *Spectator* (November 9, 1937). "Isn't it equally possible to reach a selected public with films of aesthetic interest? . . . The cinema, of course, should be a popular art, but must the popularity be worldwide?" In order to insure the financial success of a film, Greene pointed out, producers try to cater to the lowest common denominator in their potential audience by mass-producing escapist entertainment which offers no challenging ideas for the more reflective filmgoer. The average film always has a clearly defined moral, Greene wrote. "The huge public has been trained to expect a villain and a hero; and if you're going to reach the biggest possible public, it's the conflict—in terms of sub-machine guns—of the plainest Good and the plainest Evil."

In order to make the film adaptation of a novel appeal to a large number of consumers, then, the literary source may be transformed from what Greene calls a conflict of ideas to the conflict of the plainest Good and the plainest Evil.

Many inevitable differences arise between the way that a story can be presented in a novel and in a film, quite apart from the commercial considerations just mentioned. For instance, compression becomes an important factor in making a motion picture from a novel, since the novelist can take as many pages as he likes to develop his plot and characters, whereas the scriptwriter has only a couple of hours of screen time at most. One way for the screenwriter to handle this problem is to select what he considers to be the key sections of the novel and to develop them in his script to their full dramatic potential, rather than to try to present, survey-fashion, all of the events of the book.

Erich Von Stroheim proved once and for all that the latter method could not be used without producing a film of inordinate length, when he tried to film Frank Norris's *McTeague* paragraph by paragraph as *Greed* in 1923. "I had always been against cutting great chunks out of a novel to fit it into screen time," he once said. "Some of the world's greatest masterpieces have been hacked in this way."[5] Stroheim consequently came up with a film that would have been close to ten hours in running time had it been released as he made it. So, instead of great chunks being cut out of the novel when it was adapted for the screen, great chunks were cut out of the finished film by the studio.

Screenwriter Edward Anhalt, on the other hand, compressed Morton Thompson's huge novel *Not as a Stranger* into a manageable length for filming by literally tearing out of the novel the pages that constituted the episodes which he wanted to portray in the film and stringing them across a clothesline. Then he devised expository scenes that would serve as transitions from one incident to the next. Hence, his screenplay or the 1955 film was quite effective.

Commenting on the necessity of compressing a novel for the screen, producer Jerry Wald *(The Long Hot Summer)* wrote, "The watchword of all screenwriters is *economy*. . . . The screen adapter may have to delete a favorite passage or character; but he does not do so in ignorance, nor through lack of judgment, and certainly not from lack of respect for the original. He does it for creative economy."[6]

While compression is a crucial factor in adapting a novel to the screen, expansion is an important factor in adapting a short story to the screen. Consequently, adapting a short story for film represents more of a form of artistic creation for the screenwriter, than does adapting a novel for film, since adapting a short story involves addition, while adapting a novel involves subtraction. Thus the screenwriter can add scenes to a screenplay derived from a short story which serve to fill in the background of the principal characters—to a degree that was not possible within the limits of the short story format—so that we can know them better.

Screenwriter A. E. Hotchner *(Hemingway's Adventures of a Young Man)* describes the task of adapting a work of fiction to the screen as a perilous high-wire act. Adaptation by its very nature, he explains, forces the screenwriter "to deal with people not his own, set against backgrounds not of his invention. With varying degrees of success the adapter tries to identify with these people, but he does not always succeed, for it is like adopting a full-grown orphan."[7] By the same token, in expanding a short story into a full-length film, Hotchner continues, the scriptwriter must so compose the invented scenes that they will preserve the spirit of the material which inspired them, avoiding the creation of any situation or character which seems out of keeping with the tone or style of the original author's work. "A screenwriter is at best a stylistic chameleon," adds screenwriter Philip Dunne *(How Greene was My Valley);* "he writes in the style of the original source—or should, if he's worth his salt."[8]

An excellent example of expanding the plot of a short story into a full-length feature is the movie version of Hemingway's "The Killers," released in 1946. In the film, as in the short story, two Chicago gangsters invade a small town to murder a fugitive named Andreson, who has been hiding from them there. The original story does not disclose the reason why the two killers are after Andreson. But the screenwriters, Anthony Veiller (and John Huston, uncredited), expanded the short story by depicting in flashback the background of the central character, and in this way explained why he was killed.

In summary, the screenplay for the film version of "The Killers" expands the plot of the original short story in a most adroit fashion. We shall have a chance to examine the expansion of a Conrad short story into a feature-length film when we take up *Laughing Anne,* the film version of "Because of the Dollars."

In the last analysis, says George Bluestone in *Novels into Film,* what the scriptwriter is really composing is a kind of paraphrase of the fictional work which he is adapting to the screen. The resulting film, therefore, can never be a replica of the literary source on which it is based; for a work of art that was originally conceived in terms of the techniques of one medium always resists, to some extent at least, being converted into another medium. In a similar vein, Giddings, Selby, and Wensely, in their 1990 book *Screening the Novel,* cite Brian McFarlane, who stresses the "sheer improbability that an illusion of reality created in one form (i.e., the novel) could be recreated in another (i.e., film) . . . without major change."[9]

Bluestone continues: "Like two intersecting lines, novel and film meet at a point and then diverge. At the intersection, the book and the shooting script are almost indistinguishable. But where the lines diverge, they . . . lose all resemblance to each other," for each works within the framework of its own conventions.[10] For example, "there is no literary equivalent for 'getting things into the same shot,'" as Charles Barr has very perceptively pointed out. It might take a novelist several phrases to build up a description of a given object or incident, whereas the film maker can show the same thing on the screen in a single image. Vladimir Nabokov notes this in having the narrator of *Lolita* remark that there is no way for him to relay to the reader the impact he felt at seeing his wife lying dead on the street after having been struck down by a car; for he must describe the details of the scene one by one; whereas he saw the whole thing in a single flash of vision. Stanley Kubrick in his film of *Lolita* (1962) was able to show the accident in a single shot, just as the husband saw it.[11] In summary, as Giddings, Selby, and Wensley comment, "Film is very good at conveying considerable information and detail in a short space."[12]

Novelist-screenwriter William Faulkner was very much aware of the intrinsic difference between fiction and film as two separate modes of artistic expression. "You can't say the same thing with a moving picture as you can with a book," Faulkner once told an interviewer, "any more than you can express with paint what you can with plaster. The media are different."[13] Because the nature of fiction and of film, as two different media of artistic expression, are disparate, a novel "resists" translation to the screen, to use Bluestone's phrase, already quoted.

As Wald notes, "Screen adapting involves translating ideas from one *medium* to another. The novelist can spend a chapter or more to describe what is going on in the mind of his hero. He can spend paragraphs . . . to tell his reader that the hero is making up his mind."[14] But it is difficult for the screenwriter to take the filmgoer inside the mind of a character in the way that a novelist can. And therein lies the fundamental problem of bringing Conrad's fiction to the screen. For Conrad by nature was a storyteller accustomed to constructing scenes on the printed page which could not easily be transferred to the screen.

For example, he created passages that detail a character's subjective reflections on the events in which he was taking part in the story. And, as film scholar Edward Murray has noted, it is nearly impossible for film makers to "find adequate technical means" for duplicating or even approximating these subtly nuanced interior monologues in a film. [15]

Avrom Fleishman describes how filmmakers try to approximate interior monologues of the kind that Conrad employs in his fiction when adapting a novel for film. "Some films," he writes, accompany their images "with the words of a narrator who exudes the implication that this speaking is the source of what we see and hear." The narrator, in these internal monologues, recounts "the past as it later seems to a reminiscing participant." [16] Unfortunately, these attempts to recreate on the screen Conrad's interior monologues, in which a character expresses his subjective thoughts and feelings about his experiences past and present, can sound very artificial and pretentious when verbalized by an actor on the sound track.

Admittedly, certain elements of Conrad's fiction might, at first glance, appear to recommend themselves for screen adaptations, despite the difference between the two media. His novels often take place in colorful, even exotic locales. His episodic plots are easily modified; his boldly drawn characters are generally caught in an emotional crisis with which filmgoers can easily identify; and his stories are more often than not melodramatic enough to grip a movie audience's attention. Nevertheless, as we have just seen in considering the interior monologues that are characteristic of his fiction, any affinity between Conrad's fiction and the movie medium is purely superficial. In brief, the story of a Conrad work is easy to put on film, its deeper implications are not. Bruce Bawer puts it this way: "One is constantly aware," when watching a film derived from the work of a major novelist like Conrad, "that there are levels of thought and action and resonance, worked out in some artistic dimension larger than that of the film, toward which the film itself can only point." [17]

The challenging remarks of the critics just cited about the critical problems associated with filming Conrad's work indicate the rich lode to be mined by a film scholar in an examination of Conrad's films.

Although a work of fiction must admittedly undergo many superficial alterations in dialogue and plot when it is transformed into a movie, these changes must not depart in any significant fashion from the basic intent of the original author. The faithful screen adaptation, then, is one that remains essentially true to the original author's personal vision; that is, the latter's basic view of the human condition, as expressed in the work to be filmed. As Philip Dunne said, if the screenwriter "can, in a radically different medium, express the intent of the novelist, if he can capture the spirit and the inner essence . . . of the original, then he has done his work well."[18] If, on the other hand, the fundamental intent of the literary work is somehow mislaid between page and screen, then the author of the source story has just grounds for complaint.

And that brings us to another fundamental problem in bringing a Conrad story to the screen, in addition to the one already mentioned. The faithful adaptation of a Conrad work to the screen must consequently be designed to capture on film the thematic meaning—i.e., the essential spirit—of the source story.

Conrad's thematic vision centers on the Judeo-Christian concept that one achieves redemption by sacrifice and suffering. As John Lester points out in his book on Conrad and religion, Conrad's earliest religious background was that of Polish Catholicism; and while Conrad was not a practicing Catholic most of his life, "he never revoked his faith," Lester states; "and he did indeed receive a Catholic burial on his death."[19] As a matter of fact, his younger son John remembered Conrad observing to him one day when they visited a Catholic church together, "Don't assume that because I do not go to church that I do not believe; I do."[20]

Despite the fact that Conrad never pretended to present a coherent religious philosophy in his work, then, one is nevertheless right in calling him a profoundly religious writer, whose characters accordingly operate in a Judeo-Christian environment, and—regardless of their personal shortcomings—represent a spiritual concern with sacrifice and redemption. As we shall see later, the sound version of *Lord Jim* retains the spirit of Conrad's novel by retaining the tragic ending of the original tale, wherein the title character redeems an act of cowardice by facing death bravely at the end of the film. In his Foreword to this book, Graham Greene raises the issue of the possibility of translating Conrad's dark, implacable vision to a popular art form. In brief, Conrad's dark vision survives in most of the films based on his fiction, no matter how much tampering has been done with the original story in the course of its metamorphosis from book to movie.

Hollywood versus the Novelist

Given the risks that a novelist like Conrad runs in entrusting his work to a film studio for adaptation to the screen, why do so many writers willingly allow their cherished works to be filmed? For one thing, many a novelist sees the cinema as a way of making his work more available to present and future audiences that far exceed in number those who will ever read his books.

But the most obvious answer to this question is the considerable amount of income which a writer derives from selling his work to the movies. Interestingly enough, Conrad sold the American screen rights to his fiction on a single afternoon in 1919, primarily, as he was the first to admit, for the substantial increment to his income that the movie sales of his works would bring. Moreover, he had no inclination to involve himself in the making of any of the films based on his work.

John Updike, like Conrad, sees the sale of the film rights of his fiction to the movies as a source of income; and he too has hesitated to involve himself in the film making process; for there is no guarantee that a film made from one of his novels will be faithful to his original story. "Movie makers, like creative spirits everywhere, must be free; they owe nothing to the authors of the books they adapt to the screen except the money they pay them," says Updike. Consequently, he adds, the author must be content to "take the money and run."[21]

Graham Greene once wrote that the author of the work that is filmed is the "forgotten man" in the making of a movie, and pictures himself as a bewildered figure who materializes at the studio to watch the rough cut of a film drawn from his writings, clearing his throat nervously at hearing lines that are not his, but for which he will probably bear the critics' blame. The excitement of his original creation, he finds, has been lost in the many rewritings of the screenplay; and now he is the only one of the spectators who fondly remembers how it all began in his typewriter.[22]

As far as Ernest Hemingway was concerned, the best way for a writer to deal with the film industry was to arrange a rendezvous at the California border with the movie men who wanted to purchase a story: "You throw them your book, they throw you the money; then you jump into your car and drive like hell back the way you came."[23] This was Hemingway's way of saying that the fiction writer should not participate in the making of a film from one of his stories, so he can disclaim any responsibility for the finished film if it turns out badly.

Hemingway believed that a film maker is incapable of making a faithful adaptation of a fictional work because the film maker spends too much time "looking through the camera lens" when he makes a film; "all he is thinking of is pictures," said Hemingway, when he ought to be "thinking about people."[24] For his part, F. Scott Fitzgerald was himself well aware of the crucial differences between fiction and film as two separate media of artistic expression. "A writer's instinct is to think in words," he once wrote; whereas a film maker, on the other hand, must "turn the writer's words into visual images for the camera."[25]

Hence, as Fitzgerald suggests, a movie adapted from a fictional work will never be a literal transcription of the literary source from which it was derived. As *New York Times* writer Michiko Kakutani points out, the change of medium demands, among other things, subtle alterations of language. "Dialogue that seems artless on the page may sound stilted and contrived when spoken by actors." Thus a beautifully written passage, filled with stylized wordplay, may not work as well on the screen as it did in the book, because "the explicitness of film tends to turn metaphor and symbol into fact."[26] To give one salient example of Kakutani's point, Conrad meant Peter Willems's pursuit of the native girl Aïssa in *An Outcast of the Islands* to epitomize his total moral degradation. But there is a danger that Conrad's intent might conceivably be reduced on the screen merely to a white man's fancy for a pretty native girl. (For more on the actual film of *Outcast,* see Chapter 4.)

A film maker must therefore try to rethink in visual terms the literary source he is bringing to the screen by seeking to find visual equivalents for what a fiction writer has expressed in literary language, rather than attempt to maintain a slavish fidelity to the printed text of the original work. Thus Vladimir Nabokov never had anything but good comments to make about Stanley Kubrick's 1962 film of his novel *Lolita,* already mentioned, precisely because he realized the necessity of altering a fictional work for the screen. "Infinite fidelity may be the author's ideal," said Nabokov, "but can prove the producer's ruin."[27]

Director John Schlesinger vividly realized the need for altering a fictional work for film when he made a movie of Thomas Hardy's *Far from the Madding Crowd* (1967). Specifically, Schlesinger feels that he did not adapt Hardy's novel with sufficient freedom. "I was dealing with a considerable classic, which, looking back on it, I regarded with too much awe," he explains.[28] As things turned out, Schlesinger found that Hardy's superficial characters and melodramatic plot just did not work on film. Accordingly, Schlesinger resolved to allow himself more creative freedom the next time he made a film adaptation of a classic novel, by being more "irreverent" in interpreting a hallowed literary work for the cinema. Giddings, Selby, and Wensley state this point more emphatically: "The fact is and should be admitted, that filmmakers . . . have their own goals and imperatives, and that the cry of being 'true to the text' is not defensible, and need not be defended."[29]

Peter Brook, who has filmed stories by Golding and Proust, adds, "I lost my inhibitions about film literature long ago. The only way to be faithful is to be unfaithful. . . . One must create a new work of art that stands on its own as a movie; otherwise all one has done is strung together a series of dead photographs that illustrate a text like Nineteenth Century engravings.[30] The director's only constraint, Brook concludes, is to be true to the author's personal vision, as noted before; that is, the latter's fundamental conception of the human condition, as it is embedded in the work of his that is to be filmed.

In sum, the faithful adaptation is one which captures the author's personal vision—the spirit and theme of the original work. Significantly, the quotation from F. Scott Fitzgerald found at the beginning of this Introduction indicates that Fitzgerald realized the importance of preserving the *spirit* of a fictional work when it is filmed.

It follows that a film maker must respect the spirit and the theme of the material he is filming, even to the extent of consciously tailoring his personal directorial style to the demands and specifications of the tale he is translating to the screen. That is not to say that the personal style of the director is not important, since he remains ultimately responsible for the overall quality and artistic unity of the movie version of the novel he is filming. But a faithful rendition of a novel on film does require that he adapt his directorial style to the exigencies of the story which he is narrating on film. As director Richard Brooks *(Lord Jim)* has remarked, a film maker has nothing to direct until he has a story to tell.

As a matter of fact, Fitzgerald believed that the director was the heart and soul of a motion picture, to the extent that he predicted that the artistic level of motion pictures would rise only when better directors were developed in the industry. To that extent the artistic level of most of the Conrad films is very high indeed, since some of the most distinguished directors in film history have accepted the challenge of bringing Conrad's fiction to the screen. From Victor Fleming, John Cromwell, and Alfred Hitchcock to Carol Reed, Richard Books, Francis Coppola, and Ridley Scott—the list reads like a who's who of major directors.

That the nature of the relationship between fiction and film is still a live issue has been reflected in comments prompted by round table discussions of this topic at various conferences which I have attended. There are those, I have learned, who believe very strongly that literature and film should preserve their own respective turfs and be studied separately, without any attempt to understand one medium in the light of the other. My own conviction is that what one learns about the integration of literature and film as complimentary media enhances one's appreciation of both.

In examining the films of Conrad's fiction I hope to show how the wedding of fiction and film works out in practice by studying the films derived from the fiction of one writer. As I indicated at the outset, like any marriage, there have been periods of disappointment as well as of satisfaction. But when one considers all of the film versions of Conrad's fiction, one sees how generally fruitful the alliance of fiction and film can really be.

Indeed, once we have examined the many films of Conrad's fiction, I am confident that it will become clear that every one of them retains at least some moments that reflect Conrad's original work, and that at least some of them—for example, *An Outcast of the Islands* and *The Duellists*—rank as examples of superior cinema, just as the stories from which they were adapted rank as superior fiction.

Chapter 1

Exiled in Paradise:
The Early Silent Films

Although this book does not purport to be a full-dress biography of Joseph Conrad, it is appropriate to take a brief look at the private world in which Conrad grew up. For, as Tennessee Williams has observed, a writer's life is his work and his work is his life. Furthermore, Conrad often drew on his personal experiences and his observations of others in order to create fictional characters and situations in his stories, as I shall have occasion to point out throughout this book.

Jozef Teodor Korzeniowski was born in the Polish Ukraine on December 3, 1857, to Apollo Korzeniowski and Ewa Brobowska. (For simplicity's sake, I shall refer to him throughout this study by the pen name he later adopted, Joseph Conrad.) Joseph's father and mother both engaged in subversive activities designed to urge the overthrow of the Russian regime in Poland; and as a result of these activities both of his parents were exiled to Northern Russia on May 9, 1862. They were, of course, accompanied by their only child Joseph. His mother died of tuberculosis on April 18, 1865. Father and son were released from exile in January, 1868, and moved to Cracow, where Apollo died of tuberculosis on May 23, 1869.

When he was still in his teens young Joseph advised his Uncle Thaddeus, who was his guardian, that he would like to go to sea. He explained to his uncle that he was inspired in this resolve by reading the sea stories of James Fenimore Cooper and Frederick Marryat. Accordingly, he left Poland in October, 1874, at the age of sixteen, and took up residence in the port of Marseilles, serving his apprenticeship on French vessels as an ordinary seaman during the next couple of years.

Conrad eventually decided that he would like to sail on British ships, and joined the crew of his first British vessel in July 1878. In his autobiography, *A Personal Record,* Conrad notes that when he first made up his mind to be a sailor, he said to himself, "If a seaman, then an English seaman." [1] This resolve was a sensible one, since at the time that Conrad embarked on his maritime career England was mistress of the seas and clearly ruled the waves. During the next decade Conrad steadily worked himself up from the class of ordinary seaman to that of a ship's officer. The year 1886 was a significant one for him, since in November of that year he earned his diploma as a Master Mariner of the British Merchant Marine, which entitled him to a captaincy on a British vessel when one was available. Moreover, in August of that same year he officially became a British subject.

As things turned out, Conrad took command of the *Otago* in June, 1888.

Conrad began composing his first novel, *Almayer's Folly,* in September of 1889, as a way of occupying his mornings during a vacation in London that followed his commanding the *Otago* on an extended voyage to the South Seas. He continued to work on the novel off and on during the next six years while he was still pursuing his career at sea, and it was finally published in England by Unwin in 1895. Conrad had originally sent the manuscript of the novel off to Unwin in the summer of 1894, where it was read appreciatively by two of the publishing house's editors, Wilfred Chesson and Edward Garnett. It was Garnett who encouraged Conrad to pursue his writing career by moving on to the writing of his second novel. Conrad did so, and—without fully realizing it at the time—he was beginning his new career as a novelist.

Since Conrad's fiction never achieved the status of best sellers either in England or America during his lifetime, he found that selling the screen rights of his stories was an excellent way of augmenting his meager income from his literary pursuits. In his book, *My Father, Joseph Conrad,* Borys Conrad recalls that his father asked him to drive him to the American Embassy in London one summer day in June, 1919, where he completed the negotiations for the sale of the screen rights of several of his fictional works to Hollywood.[2] In a letter to his agent, J. B. Pinker, he notes that the proceeds from the sale was over £4,000.[3]

Besides selling the screen rights of his fiction to Hollywood, in order that other hands could adapt his work for film, he also made one try at writing a film scenario based on one of his works: At the request of Famous Players-Lasky (later Paramount Pictures) he composed a screenplay derived from his short story "Gaspar Ruiz" entitled *The Strong Man*. Conrad felt a bit embarrassed about writing for the cinema, since he had always considered the film medium inferior to the art of fiction. Hence he expressed this embarrassment about composing a film scenario in his correspondence. "I am ashamed to tell you this," he confided to his friend Richard Curle in a letter dated August 18, 1920, "but one must live!" Later Conrad added in a letter to Curle dated October 9 that his agent J. B. Pinker was assisting him with his task, "which seems as futile and insecure as walking on a tightrope—and at bottom much less dignified."[4]

The Strong Man: Conrad's Scenario

"Gaspar Ruiz," which is included in Conrad's collection of short stories entitled *A Set of Six*, is the tale of a simple-minded giant who becomes caught up in a South American revolution. At the climax of the story the hero leads a band of rebels in a skirmish with enemy soldiers. As Gaspar and his men besiege an enemy fort with heavy artillery, the carriage of a heavy cannon falls into a ravine. Gaspar then orders the cannon to be strapped to his stout back, so he can steady it while it fires salvos at the enemy—and as a result of his over-exertion, he falls dead at the end of the battle.

Conrad described the scenario of *The Strong Man* in a letter dated November 1, 1920 to Thomas Wise, an American collector of Conradian memorabilia, who was interested in acquiring the scenario, whether it was filmed or not: "It is in no sense a collection of notes, but a consecutive development of the story in a series of descriptions, just as the whole thing presented itself to me when I first began to think the subject out in its purely visual aspect." Then he composed a more detailed, final version of the scenario for the perusal of the studio's Story Department.

Although Zdzislaw Najder insists that no copy of the scenario of *The Strong Man* exists, the typescript of the manuscript is available at Colgate University, where the catalogue description for this item as contained in the memorabilia Joseph Conrad reads: "The script was composed before the advent of [sound in motion pictures.] Hence dialogue is reduced to the skeletal sub-title and visual narration is accordingly exploited." As Jeffrey Myers comments, the novelist conveys the story in a series of descriptive scenes that roughly follow the plot of the original story. The scenario is accordingly more descriptive than dramatic; and as Myers concludes, is thus filled with "stale phrases, windy rhetoric, and operatic melodrama."[5]

Consequently, it is not so surprising that the scenario was rejected by Famous Players-Lasky early in 1921. Nevertheless, the same studio did film the first two Conrad stories to reach the screen: *Victory* (1919) and *Lord Jim* (1925).

Since *Victory* and *Lord Jim* were both remade as talking pictures after the advent of sound in motion pictures in 1927, I shall pass over the silent versions of both novels, in order to compare each of them to the remakes that were made later on.

The next film to be based on a Conrad novel was *The Silver Treasure* (1926), derived from *Nostromo,* which will be taken up later. This was followed by *The Road to Romance* (1927), based on *Romance* and *The Rescue* (1929). Unfortunately, no copies of any of these three films are known to survive. The reason that these silent films have disappeared is that motion pictures in these early days of cinema were printed on perishable film stock; and all known copies of these films had disintegrated before copies could be transferred to permanent film stock, which later came into general use in the film industry.

The Road to Romance: The Film of Romance

The Silver Treasure was followed in 1927 by a film adaptation of *Romance,* which Conrad wrote in collaboration with Ford Madox Ford. (Ford at one point in his professional career as a writer changed his last name from Hueffer to Ford; for simplicity's sake he will be referred to in this book consistently as Ford Madox Ford.)

In 1898 Ford had invited Conrad to collaborate with him on an unfinished novel called *Serafina,* while both men continued to work on projects of their own. Conrad and his collaborator continued to labor off and on on *Romance,* as the novel eventually came to be called, until the spring of 1902, and it was finally published the following year.

In looking back on the novel at the time of publication, Conrad apportioned the authorship of the five parts into which the novel in due course came to be divided as follows: Part I, "The Quarry and the Beach," and Part V, "The Lot of Man," were largely written by Ford; Part II, "The Girl with the Lizard," was really a joint effort by both novelists; Part III, "Casa Riego," and Part IV, "Blade and Guitar," were composed entirely by Conrad alone. For the record, the film's official screen credits indicate that the scenario was based on a story by Joseph Conrad. This attribution of the film's literary source to Conrad alone was appropriate, since the film script was derived largely from Part IV, which was, by Conrad's own testimony, his work alone.

In *The Road to Romance* (1927), the film version of *Romance,* the hero was changed from an Englishman named John Kemp into a Spaniard called Don Jose Armando, so that the role could be played by MGM's Latin hearthrob, Ramon Novarro. In the film, as in the novel, the hero saves Serafina, the heroine (Marcelina Day), from having to marry the treacherous villain of the piece, whom she does not love. As the plot unfolds in the film, Serafina is then kidnapped by a gang of pirates whose leader (Marc McDermott) is infatuated with her. Don Jose in good time eventually rescues Serafina from the pirates and ultimately falls in love with her himself.

It was wise for the movie makers to confine themselves to dramatizing only one portion of the novel's plot (Part IV), for the screen, so that this material could be developed to its fullest dramatic potential in the film. This was a better approach than trying to present a survey of all the episodes in the book in a sketchy fashion, since that would have resulted in a very superficial treatment of the novel's complicated plot on the screen.

Instead, the film version of *Romance* concentrates on developing a few key incidents in the novel in full detail.

Still, *The Road to Romance* received a lukewarm reception from the critics. Thus *The New York Times* said that the production was filmed "with no little skill and inventiveness," but it is "hardly as imaginatively directed as one might hope for."[6] Other reviewers noted that the film was a handsome production, but had been tailored as a vehicle for Ramon Novarro, and as such would mostly appeal to his fans. *Victory* (1919) and *Lord Jim* (1925) were also brought to the screen during the silent period, but, as already noted, they will be discussed in tandem with their subsequent sound remakes.

The Rescue

The Rescue centers on Tom Lingard, a British seaman and trader known by the Malay natives with whom he does business as "Rajah Laut," King of the Sea. Lingard was in reality modeled on Captain William Lingard, a well-known merchant and sailor whom Conrad probably never met, but about whom he had heard a good deal of gossip during the course of his voyages in Eastern waters. Tom Lingard, the character modeled after William Lingard, had already figured in two of Conrad's earlier novels, *Almayer's Folly* and *An Outcast of the Islands*. *Outcast* was a prequel to *Almayer's Folly*, in that the principal action of the story takes place before the events narrated in *Almayer's Folly*, although it was written after *Almayer's Folly*. By the same token, *The Rescue* is a prequel to *An Outcast of the Islands*, since the events portrayed in it take place before the events chronicled in *Outcast*.

After completing the opening segment of *The Rescue*, however, Conrad lost interest in the story, and laid it aside to concentrate on projects that captured his creative imagination more strongly at the time, such as *Heart of Darkness*.

Between the time that Conrad started *The Rescue* in the late 1890's and the time he abandoned work on it in 1903, he did make sporadic efforts to work on the novel, but without success. "Now that I've got all of [the characters] together," he wrote to Garnett in June, 1896, "I don't know what to do with them." Two years later Conrad told Garnett that he was still having trouble making headway on *The Rescue:* "In the course of a working day of eight hours," he wrote to Garnett, "I write three sentences, which I erase before leaving the table in despair."[7]

Finally, in 1918, toward the end of his professional career, Conrad took *The Rescue* off the back burner and decided to complete it—perhaps because he was determined not to leave behind him any "unfinished business" when he laid down his pen for good.

The story centers on Tom's infatuation for Edith Travers, a charming lady of some breeding and social standing. The plot gets underway when the yacht on which she is travelling with her husband, a stuffy, pompous individual, is stranded just off the coast of the island where Lingard makes his home. For her part, she chafes at the boring conventionality of her marriage, and longs to become involved with an adventurous young mariner with an attractive personality like Tom. Thus Heliéna Krenn observes that Edith's "romantic inclinations are stimulated by the personality of Lingard and dispose her to respond to his appeals as she does."[8]

Tom eventually realizes, however, that he is nothing more than a passing fancy for Edith; and that she is clearly unwilling to give up the life of luxury her husband has made her accustomed to, in order to share the rough, primitive existence that constitutes Lingard's life in the outpost of civilization where he makes his home. With no little regret, but with a great deal of common sense, then, Tom accordingly renounces his love for Edith, and encourages her to return to England with her husband.

Krenn notes that Conrad's opinion of the novel underwent a change over the years. In 1897 he remarked that the novel was designed to be a glorified adventure story for boys. In 1918, when he was completing the novel, however, he reflected that the book was "not fit for juvenile readers, . . . on account of the depth and complexity of the feelings involved in the story."[9] Conrad was probably referring to Tom's mixed emotions at giving up Edith: He regrets renouncing his love for her, but is confident that it is the right thing to do.

In reviewing *The Rescue* (1929), the film version of the novel, several film critics observed that the film makers stuck closely to the film's literary source, and even retained the novel's down-beat ending, wherein Tom (Ronald Colman) and Edith (Lily Damita) reluctantly go their separate ways at the final fade-out—instead of grafting a contrived happy ending onto the movie, as was the case with *The Road to Romance.*

As it happened, *The Rescue* went into production in 1928 as a silent picture; but during the shooting period it became increasingly clear that talking pictures, which were introduced in the fall of 1927, were here to stay. As a result, the studio decided to add background music and sound effects to the film in order to give the film the flavor of a sound movie, though there was no spoken dialogue in the movie. Hence, because the film has music and sound effects, it can be called the first Conrad sound film. But Wallace Watson errs in his essay on Conrad's films when he calls *The Rescue* the first Conrad talky, simply because it had no "talk," i.e., dialogue. That distinction does apply to *Dangerous Paradise,* the first sound version of *Victory.*

Although the films dealt with in this chapter are considered lost, the balance of the movies treated in this study (except for *The Silver Treasure*) are all extant. That means that they are available for screening either on TV or through the 16mm and videocassette channels of distribution. (*Razumov,* the film adaptation of *Under Western Eyes,* was thought lost, until a print recently turned up which is now available at the Museum of Modern Art Study Center in New York.) Hence, nearly all of the films dealt with in this study are available.

Chapter 2

The Undefeated: *Victory* (1919), *Dangerous Paradise* (1930) and *Victory* (1940)

Victory: The Novel

In his "Author's Note" to *Victory* in the Collected Edition, Conrad recalls the real-life counterparts of the principal characters of the novel. He indicates that it was while serving as a steward aboard the *Saint-Antoine* in the summer of 1876 that he encountered the individual who inspired the character of Axel Heyst, the hero of *Victory*. He was a "mysterious Swede," said Conrad; and that is just what Heyst came to be in the book. Conrad is quick to add that this individual was not the whole Heyst as he envisioned him in the story, however; "he was only the physical and moral foundation of my Heyst, laid on the ground of a short acquaintance."[1]

In a letter dated June 3, 1917, Conrad added that he gained an impression of the individual who was the inspiration of his central character from observing him for a couple of hours in St. Thomas, West Indies, one of the ports of call of his voyage on the *Saint-Antoine*. "There was some talk of him after he left our party," Conrad concludes; "but all I heard of him might have been written down on a cigarette paper." Except for those hints, the fictional Axel Heyst was altogether "invented."[2]

As for Mr. Jones, the arch villain of *Victory*, Conrad encountered the individual who was to be the model of that character in the course of the same voyage. It was in a small hotel on the island of St. Thomas in 1876, Conrad writes in his "Author's Notes" to *Victory*, that he noticed him "one hot afternoon, extended on three chairs, all alone in the loud buzzing of flies, to which his immobility and his cadaverous aspect gave a most gruesome significance." Shortly afterwards the man rose, "turned his back on me, and walked out of the room. . . . I never saw him again."

In the very same year of 1876, Conrad came across the real-life counterpart of Ricardo, Jones's nefarious sidekick in the novel. The man in question, writes Conrad, "was a fellow passenger of mine on board an extremely small and extremely dirty little schooner, during a four days' passage between two places in the Gulf of Mexico whose names don't matter." For the most part, this intriguing chap "lay on the deck aft as it were at my feet; . . . . now and then he would give me a glance and make the hairs of his stiff little moustache stir quaintly."

As for Lena, the heroine of the novel, Conrad says that he encountered the girl who was to serve as the model for her one evening as he "wandered in a cafe, in a town not of the tropics but in the south of France. The cafe was filled with tobacco smoke, the hum of voices, the rattling of dominoes, and sounds of strident music." The orchestra was rather smaller than the one in which Lena performs at Schomberg's hotel in the novel, and also seemed rather more "respectable" than the one in the book.[3]

With these four principal characters firmly in mind, Conrad composed *Victory*, one of the most popular novels he ever penned; indeed, it appealed to the public to the degree that it was the basis of no less than three film versions.

Axel Heyst, the hero of the novel, is a melancholy, pessimistic Swede who grew up under the influence of a cynical father who warned him not to get involved in other people's lives, since that could only lead to misery and unhappiness. Instead he urged Axel to hold himself aloof from the human comedy as much as possible. Indeed, Axel often recalls his father's conviction that "he who forms a tie is lost" (199-200).

In trying to follow his deceased father's advice in his own life, Heyst actually spends his life living on a remote tropical island called Samburan. Nevertheless, Heyst disregards his misanthropic father's warning about making commitments to others when he meets Lena on a visit to the neighboring island of

Sourabayah. Heyst is staying at the time in a hotel run by a nasty German called Schomberg, who has hired an all-girl orchestra, presided over by a conductor named Zangiacomo, to give a concert for the guests each evening after dinner. Heyst learns during the course of his sojourn at the hotel that the vile Schomberg has sexual designs on Lena, one of the girls in the band, and has tried to force his attentions on her more than once.

"As Heyst learns more about the girl," writes Carl Bennett, "he cannot defend himself from compassion for her friendless situation and from a mounting consciousness of the growing threat posed by Schomberg's unconcealed desire for her." Hence, Lena implicitly "shakes him from his detached existence, and he takes her away with him to his island," where she will be safe from the likes of Schomberg.[4] Moreover, Frederick Karl notes in his *Reader's Guide to Conrad,* that Heyst thereby becomes the living embodiment of John Donne's belief that no man is an island, totally separate from others; for there comes a time when making an emotional investment in another human being takes precedence over an individual's preference for solitude.[5]

When Schomberg learns that Lena has fled his hotel to live in seclusion with Heyst on his private island, he is outraged. Indeed, he views Heyst's taking Lena away from him as a theft, and determines to get even with Heyst for taking Lena from him in whatever way he can. Catharine Rising comments that Schomberg "never forgives Heyst for the conquest of Lena, who embodied to a forty-five-year-old man a promise of rejuvenation."[6] The instrument of Schomberg's revenge on Heyst turns out to be three desperadoes named Jones, Ricardo, and Pedro, who show up to stay at the hotel shortly after Lena has disappeared with Heyst.

Jones, the leader of this group of ne'er-do-wells, is the kind of stereotypical homosexual who gives homosexuality a bad name: He is a repulsively effeminate creature who harbors a pathological hatred for the female of the species. Catharine Rising correctly observes that Conrad often symbolically associates Jones with Satan throughout the novel; indeed, "Jones's Satanic identification" is most notable in a paraphrase of Job 1:7. In this biblical passage the devil appears after "going to and fro in the earth, and from walking up and down in it."[7] Conrad makes use of this passage when Heyst tells Lena that Jones described himself as having been ejected "from his proper social sphere because he had refused to conform to certain usual conventions"; i.e., he had been presumably pursuing a homosexual life style. Accordingly, Jones characterized himself as "a rebel now, and was coming and going up and down the earth" (317-18).

Ricardo, the Cockney whom Jones refers to as his secretary, is a sly, cunning type, who always follows Jones's orders when they suit his purposes. Finally, there is Pedro, the third member of this nefarious trio, a sub-human brute, who seems devoted to Jones and serves as a kind of factotum for him.

Upon the arrival of Jones and his cohorts at his hotel, Schomberg hatches a plot whereby he can wreak vengeance on Heyst for depriving him of Lena. He tells Jones that Heyst has accumulated a great deal of wealth in recent years and has hidden it somewhere on his island retreat. Jones and his henchmen accordingly decide to visit Samburan and relieve Heyst of his buried treasure. Schomberg, quite aware that no such treasure exists, will thus get even for the injustice he thinks Heyst has done him by siccing Jones and his gang on Heyst; for Schomberg knows that Jones will stop at nothing, including torture and murder, to force Heyst to disclose the whereabouts of his fabled riches.

When Jones and the others arrive on Heyst's island, Ricardo is the first to notice the presence of Lena, of whom Schomberg made no mention when he spoke to Jones and his co-conspirators about Heyst and his treasure. Ricardo fears that Jones will abandon his plan to stay on Samburan until he has gotten hold of Heyst's wealth, if he discovers that there is a female living there. Hence he "neglects" to mention Lena's presence to his boss.

Matters come to a head when Jones threatens Heyst with his life if he does not hand over his hidden treasure to him, since he refuses to listen to Heyst's protestations that no such treasure exists. At this crucial moment Lena comes forth in order to stand by Heyst, and Jones is beside himself when he learns that Ricardo knew about her existence all along and failed to tell him about her. Jones reasons that Ricardo is no longer a trustworthy confederate. After all, if the crafty Ricardo can deceive his boss once, he very likely will do so again. And so Jones simply decides to dispose of Ricardo by shooting him.

Meanwhile Ricardo, who mistakenly sees Lena as his ally, confides to her his intention to kill Heyst, once Heyst has divulged the whereabouts of his treasure. Lena accordingly possesses herself of Ricardo's trusty knife through a clever ruse, since she believes that, in disarming him, she is protecting the life of the man she loves. At this point, Jones comes upon the pair; and in his determination to kill Ricardo he shoots at him. But he misfires and accidentally wounds Lena instead. For his part Wang, Heyst's paranoid Chinese houseboy, has harbored a fear of Jones's brutish servant Pedro from the very first time he laid eyes on him. Wang therefore allays his fears of Pedro by murdering him. In addition, Jones shoots at Ricardo a second time and this time his bullet finds its mark.

Jones has now lost both of his partners in crime, and presumably comes to feel that his plans to possess Heyst's legendary treasure have come to nought. Therefore he apparently drowns himself at the seashore in despair. As a matter of fact, Conrad does not specify whether or not Jones dies a suicide. He simply has one of the characters observe, "Then, apparently, Jones went down to the wharf to look for the boat. . . . I suppose he tumbled into the water by accident—or perhaps not by accident" (411). I prefer to think that Jones drowned himself deliberately, for the reasons given.

As things turn out, Jones's stray bullet has wounded Lena mortally; and she dies, serene in the belief that her love of Axel Heyst will conquer death. Heyst is despondent at the loss of the only person who has ever loved him; and her death drives him to suicide. And so he sets fire to his living quarters, so that he can be united with Lena in the world to come. Now that he knows what true love is, Heyst is able to declare before he dies, "Woe to the man whose heart has not learned while young to hope, to love" (410). "Heyst's choice of fire," says Rising, "might indicate a yearning for the emotional warmth he has repressed or lacked" all his life.[8]

It is evident from the body count at novel's end that, despite its implicitly optimistic title, *Victory* is one of Conrad's darkest novels. For it ends with the death of all of the major characters, from the hero and the heroine to Jones and his villainous band. Nevertheless, given the novel's exciting, melodramatic plot, it is no surprise that Paramount opted to bring the novel to the screen.

Victory (1919): The Silent Film of Victory

The silent version of *Victory* opened in November, 1919, and hence was the only Conrad film produced during the author's lifetime, though there is no indication that he actually saw the picture. It received mainly favorable notices, with much praise going to director Maurice Tourneur and his distinguished cast. Schomberg is played by Wallace Beery *(Dinner at Eight);* Alma, the heroine, by Seena Owen *(Intolerance);* Ricardo by Lon Chaney (the screen's first Phantom of the Opera); and Heyst by Tim Holt. The script was by Stephen Fox, a pseudonym for the distinguished screenwriter Jules Furthman *(The Big Sleep).*

"Tourneur was most literate in his pronouncements on the cinema," writes Liam O'Leary. He cites Tourneur as saying that "it costs a great deal of money to produce a motion picture. The only way the financial backer can get his money back, to say nothing of a profit, is to appeal to the great masses."[9] Tourneur managed to reach the mass audience with his skillfully made film of *Victory.*

(It will be noted that the heroine's name is listed as Alma in the cast list above. Lena is Alma's nickname in the book, while Alma is used as the name of the heroine in all three films.)

A printed prologue opens the film; it reads: "Samburan, the island of our tale, was a lonely desert outpost in the Dutch East Indies. It was here that Axel Heyst, for reasons best known to himself, had lived in complete, impregnable solitude. His only visitors were shadows, the shadows of a life foresworn, drawn from the books of his father, a writer of great vision and charm."

The prologue establishes the profound influence which Heyst's father has had on him, an influence which has encouraged him to go through life as a spectator who declines to get involved with others. Heyst is slowly drawn out of his solitude, however, when he brings Alma to his island; and he is stirred into action when he is forced to cope with Jones and his criminal companions.

Tourneur and Furthman have made an interesting departure from Conrad's story which is worth mentioning. It comes about in the film when Pedro burns Jones to death, whereas Jones drowns himself in the book. The script supplies the motivation for Pedro's murder of Jones in a flashback which is derived from an episode in the book. In the novel Jones refers to this incident while talking with Schomberg: "Shall I tell you how I killed [Pedro's] brother in the wilds of Colombia? Well perhaps some other time—it's rather a long story. What I shall always regret is that I didn't kill him, too. I could have done it without any extra trouble then. Now it's too late" (104).

The flashback shows that sometime back Jones ruthlessly burned one of his henchmen to death by pushing him into a campfire when the latter rebelled against Jones's dictatorial ways. The victim, it turns out, was in reality Pedro's brother; and Pedro has been biding his time ever since, waiting for the opportunity to get even with Jones for his brother's painful death. And so, when Pedro sees Jones firing at Ricardo at the film's climax, he growls at him, "You have killed too much; maybe you don't kill any more." Pedro ties Jones up in a chair in Heyst's living room and then dumps him face-forward into the fireplace, where the blazing flames reduce Jones to ashes—thus dispatching Jones in exactly the same manner in which Jones had destroyed Pedro's hapless brother.

O'Leary begins his essay on Tourneur by calling him "one of the greatest pictorialists of the cinema."[10] Certainly Tourneur's knack for visual imagery is very much on display in this film; as a matter of fact, the director was at pains to incorporate into the film some of the visual imagery from the book. For example, in both book and film there is a volcano on a nearby island that can be seen throughout the film, smouldering in the distance. One of the printed inter-titles describes the volcano this way: "Night came with heavy stealth, bringing a dreadful murk, broken now and then by the infernal glare of the pit." During the course of the film's bloody climax the volcano finally erupts into a thundering explosion, which symbolically parallels the outburst of violence on Heyst's island when Jones forces a showdown with him.

After the film was released, there was some disappointment rightly expressed in critical circles that the movie's altered ending departed considerably from the book's conclusion. In the film Jones misfires when he shoots at Ricardo, after learning that Ricardo has deceived him about the presence of a woman on the island. He does not, however, kill Alma accidentally with the bullet meant for Ricardo, as he does in the novel. Alma therefore remains alive at the end of the picture, as does Heyst. This altered ending of the film of course, allows the hero and the heroine to gallop off into the sunset, as it were, thereby creating a happy ending for the movie that runs counter to Conrad's clear intentions in the book.

Still, although Tourneur's film of *Victory* has a contrived upbeat ending which is at odds with the novel's grim finale, all in all the silent version of *Victory* is a creditable adaptation of the Conrad original. It is a film which found favor with both the critics and the mass audience. Little wonder, then, that Paramount decided to remake the movie as a talky after the advent of sound.

Dangerous Paradise (1930): The Second Film of Victory

The talky version of *Victory* was released in 1930, and hence Frederick Karl is wrong when he suggests in his biography of Conrad that two film versions of the novel were produced in Conrad's lifetime, since the second film did not appear until six years after Conrad's death.[11] As in the case of the silent version of *Victory,* one could not complain about the cast that was assembled for the movie. Richard Arlen *(Wings)* plays Heyst and Nancy Carroll, one of Paramount's top leading ladies at the time, plays Alma.

The *Variety* review (February 19, 1930) mentioned that the movie has no less than five villains; and they are played to the hilt by an assortment of reliable character actors. Frank Thompson singles out for special mention "the eternally weaselly Clarence H. Wilson as Zangiacomo, leader of the all-girl orchestra, and the fat and oily Warner Oland *(Shanghai Express)* . . . as the hotel owner Schomberg." Rounding out the list of villains, of course, are Jones (Gustav Von Seyffertitz), Ricardo (Francis MacDonald), and Pedro (George Kotsonaros).

It is interesting to note in perusing the opening credits of the film that the movie is said to be based on "incidents from a novel by Joseph Conrad"—without any indication of which of his novels served as the basis for the present film. Thompson speculates that this vague reference to the film's literary source in the screen credits might well have been a covert attempt on the part of the film makers to "deflect criticism from the rather cavalier treatment of Conrad's novel" in the movie.[12] Cavalier is not a strong enough term to characterize the way that the film departs from the novel.

The movie begins with a printed prologue which suggests that Sourabayah, the island where Schomberg's hotel is located, is a haven for villains like the ones mentioned above. The prologue cites Kipling's poem, "The Road to Mandalay," as follows:

"Somewhere east of Suez,
Where the best is like the worst,
Where there ain't no Ten Commandments,
And a man can raise a thirst . . ."

The prologue concludes, "It must have been Sourabayah of which Kipling wrote." Certainly Mr. Jones, among the individuals who pass through Sourabayah in the course of the film, would agree that, as far as he is concerned, "there ain't no Ten Commandments."

Soon after the prologue we see Alma's first meeting with Heyst at the hotel; during their conversation she learns of his intention to return to his private island of Samburan that night. In this scene Heyst confides to Alma the reason why he has chosen to live apart from the world at large. His motive in the book for sequestering himself on Samburan, we remember, was to heed his father's warning that making commitments to other human beings is lethal. The explanation he offers Alma in the movie for living alone, however, is that he is bitter over a previous love affair, which turned out badly. As he expresses himself laconically to Alma, "I loved a girl once, too much." Wallace Watson comments on Heyst's remark in his essay on the films that the influence of Heyst's skeptical father on his withdrawal from human contact is thus transformed into romantic cliché.

Next the film establishes Schomberg and Zangiacomo's rivalry for Alma's favors; in fact, both men try to seduce her in the course of the evening. Wellman introduces an interesting visual symbol into the scene in which Alma subsequently shuts herself in her cell-like bedroom in the hotel, in order to escape the unwanted attentions of both men. As she lies on her bed crying, she is photographed through the bars of the bedstead, which make her look like a prisoner lying on a cot in a cell. This image implies how she is imprisoned in a wretched existence from which she yearns to escape. In fact, she does escape her prison shortly afterwards by fleeing with Heyst to his island paradise that same night.

Wellman then portrays a scene that was invented for the film. In this scene it is clear from the outset that neither Schomberg nor Zangiacomo are aware that Alma has left Sourabayah with Heyst, and hence both men converge on her room, hoping to find her there. Much to their chagrin, they only encounter each other. In a fit of rage Schomberg decides to get rid of his rival once and for all. He therefore murders Zangiacomo, a drastic step he does not take in the novel.

Wellman thereupon photographs the killing in a striking way. As Schomberg advances menacingly toward Zangiacomo, the latter picks up a large candlestick with which to defend himself. Then the candle falls from the holder and lies, still lit, on a bureau. Instead of cutting to a shot of the two adversaries grappling in a death struggle, Wellman holds the camera on a close-up of the burning candle. Just as we hear Zangiacomo scream off-camera, followed by the sound of his body tumbling down a staircase, we see the flame of the candle go out. This visual image symbolizes how Schomberg has snuffed out his victim's life as if he were extinguishing the wick of a candle.

As Schomberg stares at Zangiacomo's corpse at the foot of the stairs, ominous shadows fall across the body. He looks up to see Jones, along with his deadly companions, asking to register in the hotel. After Schomberg learns that Alma has gone off to Heyst's island, he hopes to avenge himself on Heyst for taking Alma from him by encouraging the desperadoes to go after Heyst for his supposed fortune.

At this point Wellman introduces another scene not in the novel, one which centers on the murder of Schomberg. Jones advises Schomberg that he intends to go after Heyst's treasure, but he coolly adds, "We have no intention of trusting you." With that, Jones gives the nod to Pedro, who yanks Schomberg off-screen. Ricardo lights Jones's cigarette as they listen nonchalantly to Schomberg's scream for mercy—a plea that goes unheeded.

One can accept the first murder which the screenwriters have added to the plot as sufficiently motivated, since Schomberg kills Zangiacomo to rid himself of the man who is competing with him for Alma. But the motivation for the second killing that has been added to the story is harder to explain. Jones never discloses the exact reason why he does not trust Schomberg and hence wants him dead. Perhaps the murder is, then, an act of pure sadism. Ricardo, after all, had said to Schomberg earlier that Jones and his friends "prey on cats that don't have the claws to resist." Perhaps Jones views Schomberg as such a cat. Still the viewer ultimately never knows for sure what motive lies behind the slaying of Schomberg. In short, adding to the film one additional murder that is not in the source story seems acceptable, since it is clearly motivated; adding a second killing, especially one that is not plainly motivated, seems to be overloading the plot with unnecessary material.

Dangerous Paradise departs from is source story to a considerable degree. For example, after Jones and company arrive on Samburan, Ricardo makes advances on Alma, and Heyst intervenes by drawing his gun to stop him. Ricardo, in turn, reacts by pulling a knife with which to ward off Heyst's attack; but Heyst kills him before he can use the knife. In the novel, of course, Jones shoots Ricardo, and Heyst kills no one but himself.

Heyst and Alma both survive at the conclusion of the film to go on sharing their lives together, whereas they both die in the book. That Heyst and Alma live on at film's end is in keeping with the pervasive theme of Wellman's films. For, as Stephen Hanson says, "In all cases the issue is one of survival, a concept that manifests itself in some manner in all of Wellman's films."[13] Still, in imposing his frequent theme on the ending of the present picture, Wellman departed notably from Conrad's novel.

Furthermore, here is a brief summary of the more notable departures from the novel, mentioned earlier. Heyst's reason for becoming a hermit is reduced in the film to his unwillingness to get involved with another girl in the wake of his earlier sad love affair. By contrast, in the book Heyst's withdrawal from society is dictated by his father's pessimistic attitude toward life. Furthermore, Schomberg's murder seems to be a superfluous addition to the plot, since it is never adequately motivated. In addition, the arch villain Jones does not die in the film, as he does in the novel. Instead Heyst sees Jones off when he boards the boat that has stopped at Samburan to deliver the mail.

What's more, Heyst and Jones actually part friends, as Jones casually observes to Heyst that he regrets that they could not have met under better circumstances (!). This final scene in the film, in which Heyst and Jones are reconciled, is inexcusably far-fetched, and underscores just how far *Dangerous Paradise* strays from true fidelity to the Conrad novel.

Victory (1940): The Third Film of Victory

The second remake of *Victory* was directed by John Cromwell (*Since You Went Away*) in 1940. As it happened, Cromwell had wanted to direct an American stage production of *Victory* some twenty years before he directed a film adaptation of it. He wrote to J. B. Pinker, Conrad's agent, in the hope of obtaining permission to have a stage dramatization of the novel prepared, but Pinker advised him that the dramatic rights had already gone to actor-producer Basil McDonald Hastings for a British production. We do not know the date of Cromwell's letter to Pinker, but it could not have been written before 1916, the year that Conrad conceded the dramatic rights of the novel to Hastings.

Undaunted, Cromwell decided to direct an American production of the Hastings script, once Hasting's stage version was finished. Cromwell had assumed that Conrad was co-authoring the dramatization of the novel, and so negotiated for the American production rights to the play without seeing the script. When the completed script finally arrived, he was vastly disappointed with it, since it did not, in Cromwell's estimation, do justice to the novel.

Cromwell then sent Hastings a letter containing a list of his specific objections to the adaptation, which Hastings simply brushed aside. Cromwell sent a copy of the letter to Conrad, who responded that he understood Cromwell's objections to Hasting's dramatization of the book, but he hesitated to interfere with Hasting's work.

Cromwell's list of objections to the Hastings adaptation is not extant, but by all accounts Hastings diluted the serious thematic implications of Conrad's tragic novel in order to enhance its appeal to the theater-going public. Nevertheless, Conrad did not object to Hasting's approach to the play, even if Cromwell did. In a letter to Hastings, Conrad assured him that he was "quite content to trust [him] entirely with the alterations" that were necessary to adapt the novel for stage presentation. He continued by saying that Hastings need not send him a finished copy of the play, since he would just as soon wait to see the play take life and shape on stage.[14] As a matter of fact, Conrad's wife Jessie testifies that her husband declined to attend a single performance, although he might have gone to some rehearsals.

The play eventually opened on March 26, 1919, at the Globe Theater, where it ran for four-and-a-half months. Cromwell directed a production of the play in America, which, like the London production, was only moderately successful.

In any event, the dramatic version of *Victory* was not Conrad's last brush with the stage. He subsequently created his own stage adaptation of *The Secret Agent* and also composed a dramatic version of his short story "Because of the Dollars," entitled *Laughing Anne*. We shall take up both of these plays by Conrad in good time, in connection with the films made from *The Secret Agent* and "Because of the Dollars." As for Cromwell, he was delighted to have the chance to make a film of *Victory,* since he was never satisfied with Hastings's stage version of the novel.

It goes without saying that Cromwell's film version of *Victory* is more faithful to its literary source than *Dangerous Paradise* had been. This fact is accounted for, at least in part, by Cromwell's conscious determination to make a more screen-worthy adaptation of *Victory* than Wellman's film had been. As Cromwell put it, "During the first weeks of my contract at Paramount, they made a production of *Victory* entitled *Dangerous Paradise* which was just deplorable."[15] Cromwell was confident that he could do better, and so he did.

The third film of *Victory* has many pluses going for it. For instance, one cannot fault the stellar cast of the film. Heyst was played by the estimable Fredric March *(The Best Years of Our Lives)*; Alma by Betty Field *(King's Row)*; Schomberg by Sig Ruman *(A Night at the Opera)*; and Jones by Cedric Hardwicke *(Suspicion)*. The scenes skillfully shot on location in the Celebes are another plus.

Like the two films of *Victory* before it, this movie likewise opens with a printed prologue: "This is the story of a man who believed that happiness consisted in living apart from his fellow men." The prologue is followed by a dissolve to Heyst's photograph in a newspaper, with an accompanying headline which says that Heyst has gone bankrupt. Heyst is then seen entering Schomberg's hotel on Sourabayah and asking for a room. Tesman, an old friend of his, expresses his regret that Heyst's recent business venture with a man named Morrison has failed. Interestingly enough, the present film, scripted by John Balderston *(Bride of Frankenstein)*, is the only one of the three adaptations of *Victory* that we are considering which mentions Morrison, who is an important character in the book.

In the source story Heyst goes against his father's insistence that he not involve himself with others: He bails out of debt a penniless trader named Morrison by loaning Morrison money he knows will never be repaid. Heyst gets drawn further into Morrison's business affairs by becoming his partner in a coal company, which eventually goes bankrupt. The gossip instigated by Schomberg among his hotel patrons is that Heyst is entirely to blame for this financial disaster. "Heyst's response to . . . the collapse of the company, of his first venture into action and human society," literary critic Stephen Land comments, "is a yet more rigorous withdrawal."[16]

Furthermore, Heyst is embittered by the gossip circulated by Schomberg that the whole debacle is his fault. This point is made in the film when Heyst's friend Tesman tells Heyst that he deplores the fact that everyone blames him, quite unfairly, for the failure of his business venture with Morrison. Heyst replies that he is going back to Samburan, where the gossip cannot reach him.

That evening Heyst meets Alma during the intermission of the concert Zangiacomo's orchestra is giving at the hotel. When she inquires why he lives on an island, he answers, "Whenever I return to the outside world, I run into another Morrison. There must be something wrong with me." Little does Heyst realize that Alma will turn out to be "another Morrison." For, just as pity inspired Heyst to befriend Morrison, so pity will move him to rescue Alma from Schomberg's plan to make her his mistress. In fact, before the night is over, Heyst takes Alma with him to live on Samburan, his sanctuary.

Cromwell demonstrates his adroit employment of visual symbols in the film in two scenes in particular. There is, for example, the scene in which Heyst shows Alma around his house, following their arrival. He comes upon the portrait of his father and explains that his father told him on his death bed that a man who forms ties is lost. Heyst winces for a moment as he looks at his father's picture, for he is suddenly aware that, in allowing Alma to take refuge on his island, he is forming a tie. As Heyst looks up at the portrait, his father's face seems to be staring at him in disapproval; and Heyst is disconcerted by the gaze.

Another significant use of visual imagery occurs in the scene in which Jones and his entourage arrive at Schomberg's hotel. Jones is wearing sunglasses which make him look remote and mysterious—an indication that he is prone to hide his thoughts and feelings behind them. Moreover, when he removes the sunglasses at one point, he squints, as if he were not used to sunlight. This suggests that he is a sinister creature of darkness, capable of dark deeds.

As in the novel (and in the other two films of *Victory*), Jones opens a gambling casino in Schomberg's hotel, much against Schomberg's wishes, since he fears gambling will cause trouble with the police. Getting Jones to close down his casino provides Schomberg with an additional motive for coaxing the three blackguards to move on to Heyst's island and go after his legendary treasure, in addition to the motive about which we already know.

Not long after Jones arrives on Samburan, the trouble starts. Jones and Heyst quarrel about Heyst's non-existent treasure when a storm breaks out, which causes the lights to go out in the house. A scuffle ensues, in which Jones commences firing his gun at Heyst in the dark. Cromwell lights the scene solely with lightning flashes in order to create an eerie atmosphere. The lightning bolts aid Jones in picking Heyst out in the darkness, so that he can take aim at him. There is some further scuffling in the dark, Jones fires one last shot, and then there is silence. A servant brings in a lantern which reveals that Jones has gone to his well-deserved death by being pushed over a balcony by Heyst—instead of taking his own life, as in the novel.

Meanwhile Alma has stabbed Ricardo to death with his own knife, when she discovers his plan to do away with Heyst after he finds the treasure. In the book, we remember, she only disarms Ricardo, and it is Jones who kills him.

In the last scene Heyst reassures Alma that "We've won our victory." Heyst's statement indicates that the victory of the film's title refers to their vanquishing their enemies. But the title of the novel refers, in a more somber fashion, to the heroine's moral victory, wherein her devotion to her beloved Heyst will conquer death by lasting beyond the grave.

Cromwell elicited ensemble acting of a high order from his cast, and more than one critic singled out Hardwicke for his chilling performance as the vicious homosexual Mr. Jones. Typical of the praise accorded Hardwicke's portrayal was the review in *The New York Herald Tribune*: "The Hardwicke characterization of the evil, woman-hating Mr. Jones ... comes through with the impact it had in the book. Terror stalks from the first moment that Mr. Jones appears, and it builds into an irresistible crescendo," as he plots to rob "the supposedly wealthy Heyst."[17]

Considering the critical admiration of Hardwicke's handling of the role of Jones, it is rather astounding that Cromwell himself thought Hardwicke gave the only weak performance in the movie. In the same interview already cited, the director complained that Hardwicke put little effort into his playing of Jones: "I don't know what the hell happened to him," Cromwell commented.[18] For myself, I prefer to side with the critical majority, who found Hardwicke's skillfully underplayed depiction of Jones superb.

Wellman's *Dangerous Paradise* is clearly the least faithful rendition of Conrad's book. But when it comes to deciding whether the Tourneur version or the Cromwell version of the book is closer to the spirit of the Conrad original, it seems to be a toss-up, since one film sticks as close to Conrad as the other. In addition, both films have much to recommend them. For example, each dramatizes an incident from the novel that might easily have been overlooked by the film makers who made each version of the book. Thus Tourneur portrays the death of Pedro's brother and Cromwell does a scene which establishes Heyst's doomed efforts to save Morrison from bankruptcy.

Still, neither film is flawless. On the one hand, Tim Holt makes a competent Heyst in the Tourneur movie, but he does not come across as a strong leading man; on the other hand, Jerome Cowan is not nearly menacing enough as the wily Ricardo in the Cromwell film. All in all, though, both films are equally fine renditions of their common literary source.

The one flaw that all three films share in common is the contrived upbeat ending which has been grafted onto all three of these versions of Conrad's story, which Conrad would not have sanctioned, wherein the hero and the heroine survive to enjoy a long life together. The insistence of the front office at Paramount on attaching a happy ending to all three films was dictated by the fact that many producers still subscribed in those days to the belief that films with upbeat endings usually attracted a larger segment of the mass audience than films which did not. The producers saw popular tearjerkers like *Camille* (1937) as the exception that proved the rule.

Two footnotes on the films of Conrad's novel need to be mentioned. First, there is a 1981 film which bears the title *Vic-*

tory which has nothing to do with Conrad's book. Second, according to an article in *Joseph Conrad Today* (Fall, 1987), a fourth version of this venerable property was made in 1987 in Germany with Sam Waterston as Heyst and Susan Hamilton as Alma, entitled *The Devil's Paradise*. But since I have been unsuccessful in tracking down any further information on the film, I do not know whether it is more faithful to the spirit of Conrad's book than any of the previous versions examined in this chapter. One can only hope that it is.

Chapter 3

The Asphalt Jungle:
Razumov (1936) and *Sabotage* (1936)

Under Western Eyes: The Novel

Conrad was the son of a very active revolutionary, a resistance worker who advocated the violent overthrow of the Russian regime in Poland. Consequently, it seems natural that Conrad himself would have been interested in portraying in his fiction the perilous world of revolutionary spies and counterspies. In the "Author's Note" to *A Personal Record* in the Collected Edition, Conrad writes, "As a child, of course, I knew very little of my father's activities, for I was not quite twelve when he died."

Nevertheless, he did remember his father holding secret meetings in the Conrad home in Warsaw before the Russian authorities sent him and his wife and son into exile. Just about all he remembered of these meetings, says Conrad, is one room in the house, "white and crimson, probably the drawing room. In one of its walls there was the loftiest of archways."[1] Very likely, he opines, the people who passed through that archway to the room beyond were dedicated underground workers like his father and, as such, worthy of young Joseph's respect and admiration.

Conrad wrote two novels about the world of spies and anarchists, both of which were filmed in 1936: *Razumov,* which was based on *Under Western Eyes* and *Sabotage,* which was derived from *The Secret Agent.*

The first novel which we shall take up is *Under Western Eyes,* which concerns the assassination of a Russian government official by a university student who is subsequently turned over to the secret police by a fellow student. In a letter to John

Galsworthy, composed in 1908 (two years before Conrad finished the book), Conrad said that the assassination in his book
was inspired by an incident which took place in Russia in 1904.
Sasonov, a university student, killed Vyacheslav de Plehve, the
minister of state.

Conrad fictionalized these events in *Under Western Eyes,*
which tells the story of a Russian university student named
Razumov who becomes embroiled in subversive activities
against his will. The story is told through the "western eyes" of a
British professor of languages, who knew personally Razumov
and some of the other principal characters in the action. Conrad, in explaining in his "Author's Note" to the novel in the
Collected Edition his reason for employing a narrator to tell the
story to the reader, says, "In my desire to produce the effect of
actuality, it seemed to me indispensable to have an eyewitness
to the transactions."[2] Moreover, in relaying Razumov's tragic
life to the reader, the English narrator at times draws upon
Razumov's diary to fill in missing details in his narrative. The
narrator's employment of this written documentation is meant
to confirm the authenticity of his tale, since he is not merely
relying on his own memory of the events he is retelling, but on
written testimony as well.

Conrad outlined a synopsis of the plot of the novel in his letter to Galsworthy which was written during the early weeks in
which Conrad was working on the novel. The story begins, he
says, in St. Petersburg, where "the student Razumov . . . gives
up secretly to the police his fellow student Victor Haldin, who
seeks refuge in his rooms after committing a political crime
(supposed to be the murder of de Plehve)." Conrad concludes
his synopsis by saying, "The psychological developments leading
to Razumov's betrayal of Haldin" and his subsequent confession
of the fact "form the real subject of the story."[3] Keith Carabine
comments on Conrad's remark by saying that "betrayal, and the
subsequent need" either to justify or to confess it describes the
novel's fundamental theme.

The night that Haldin appears in Razumov's rooms, the latter
seeks to justify his inclination to betray Haldin to the authorities because of the resentment that he secretly feels for the fugitive. Specifically, he is angry with Haldin for gratuitously assum-

ing that he supports his revolutionary cause and will therefore protect him from the police. Razumov is also afraid that he will be open to the charge of complicity in Haldin's conspiracy if he gives him sanctuary.

The novel's narrator, the language teacher, gives us Razumov's inner thoughts at this point. Razumov saw himself captured and condemned as a co-conspirator with Haldin, "shut up in a fortress, worried, badgered, perhaps ill-used. He saw himself deported by an administrative order, his life broken, ruined, and robbed of all hope. . . . It was best to keep this man out of the streets till he could be got rid of with some chance of escaping. That was the best that could be done. Razumov, of course, felt the safety of his lonely existence to be permanently endangered. This evening's doings could turn up against him at any time. . . . He hated the man" (21).

As the evening wears on, Razumov is increasingly tempted to turn Haldin over to the secret police, a temptation which finally hardens into a bitter resolve. "I shall give him up," he tells himself. "By what bond of common faith, of common conviction, am I obliged to let that fanatical idiot drag me down with him?" (37-38) Razumov accordingly informs the secret police that Haldin has told him that he is to rendezvous at 12:30 a.m. with one Ziemianitch, who will help Haldin make his escape through the snowy night in his sleigh; and Razumov advises the police of the location of the rendezvous.

After Haldin takes his leave of Razumov in order to go and meet his cohort, Razumov removes his pocket watch from his waistcoat and places it on the table before him. He keeps checking the time, as he anxiously waits for the hands on his watch to reach 12:30, at which time Haldin will be taken into custody by the police. Conrad builds unbearable tension in this scene, as Razumov sits alone in his lodgings, wondering if Haldin's capture will go off as planned. He fears that if Haldin gives the police the slip by failing to show up for his planned rendezvous with Ziemianitch, they will suspect him of having deliberately misled them, in order to help Haldin get away.

When he suddenly realizes that his watch has stopped, he then listens for the town clock to strike. "He felt ready to swoon. The faint deep boom of the distant clock seemed to explode in his head—he heard it so clearly—One! If Haldin had not turned up the police would have been already here, ransacking the house. No sound reached him. This time it was done" (65). With great relief Razumov senses that his ordeal is over.

Razumov does not realize that his ordeal is just beginning. He is retained by the Russian secret police as an undercover agent, in the wake of his involvement in the capture and execution of Haldin, so that he may be of further use to them. Razumov is in due course sent to Geneva, a haven for Russian anarchists, to contact a group of revolutionaries who were friends of Victor Haldin—a group that includes Victor's sister Nathalie.

Razumov's decision "to be recruited as a Tsarist double agent," writes Carabine, "serves to render his existence completely false and ensures he becomes increasingly bitter and more isolated the longer he lives"[4] in what the novel describes as his "prison of lies" (363). Moreover, as Eloise Knapp Hay points out, Razumov is initially drawn to consider confessing his betrayal of Haldin to Nathalie because of his "growing disgust for the deceit he must practice on her while serving as a police spy."[5]

It is evident that Conrad revised the plot of the story as he wrote the novel, since the tentative synopsis of the plot which he gave Galsworthy differs in significant ways from the novel as we have it, once Razumov settles in Geneva. According to this early outline of the story, Razumov not only falls in love with Nathalie, but "marries her, and after a time confesses to her the part he played in the arrest of her brother."[6] Razumov is prompted to admit his cooperation in her brother's death to Nathalie, Victor's sister, in this version of the story, when he sees the marked resemblance of their child to the late Victor Haldin.

In the finished novel, however, Razumov does not marry Nathalie, much less have a son by her that looks like his uncle, though he does ultimately admit to her his role in her brother's death. Conrad was well advised not to have made Razumov's motive for confessing to Nathalie his part in Victor's death the fact that his own son looks like Victor, since that turn of events would have seemed sentimental and contrived. Having Razumov admit his guilt to Nathalie, and later to Haldin's fellow revolutionaries, simply because he wants to cleanse his conscience of the guilt he feels for having been party to Victor's execution, is a much more compelling and creditable way of handling this material.

In the novel as it stands Razumov's growing sense of guilt is portrayed throughout the story. There is, for example, what Roderick Davis terms "the agonized scene where he—whom Nathalie does not yet know to be the betrayer of her brother—has just broken the news to her that Victor has now been executed." His sense of guilt is here reflected in "observing the sister's awful suffering as a result of this disclosure," an anguish that he has caused by being responsible for her brother's death.[7]

When Razumov reveals his role in Haldin's execution to Haldin's co-resistance workers in the novel, they punish him by having one of their number, Nikita by name, puncture his eardrums. Conrad portrays this scene very graphically, to put it mildly. "Three men held him pinned against a wall," while he "received a tremendous blow on the side of his head over the ear. . . . Razumov could struggle no longer. He was exhausted; he had to watch passively the open hand of the brute descend again in a degrading blow over his other ear. It seemed to split his ear in two." Razumov's torturers then "flung him out into the street" (368-69).

Nikita exults with horrible glee, "Razumov! He shall never be any use as a spy on anyone. He wont' talk because he will never hear anything in his life—not a thing. I have burst the drums of his ears for him" (371). Nikita has thereby plunged Razumov into a world of silence and isolation for the rest of his days.

Razumov: The Film

The movie version of *Under Western Eyes,* a French film directed by Marc Allégret (*Lady Chatterly's Lover,* 1955), was made in 1936. It was entitled *Razumov,* which was the working title of the novel. Its leading players were among the best French actors of their generation. Razumov is played by Pierre Fresnay (*Grand Illusion*), Victor Haldin by Jean-Louis Barrault (*Children of Paradise),* and Laspara, Haldin's close friend, by Michel Simon *(La Chienne).*

Allégret dispenses with the British narrator of the book, who tells the story in flashbacks, and simply allows the plot of the film to unfold for the viewer in chronological order. The novel is divided into four parts. Part One has St. Petersburg for its locale and deals with Razumov's betrayal of Haldin. The last three sections of the book take place in Geneva and portray Razumov's association with the resistance workers who were Haldin's friends, as well as with his relationships with several other Russian expatriates.

The first two-thirds of the film focus on Part One of the novel, which is set in St. Petersburg, while the last third of the film represents a condensation of the last three sections of the book which are set in Geneva. This condensation of the Geneva material is accomplished in the movie by limiting the narrative essentially to Razumov's interaction with the band of co-revolutionists, and eliminating from the Geneva segment of the film virtually all of the characters in the book who are not allied somehow with the terrorist group.

The film starts with a wordless scene that depicts in purely visual terms Haldin's assassination of the minister of state. Allégret's camera peers through the window of a government building from the outside, and focuses on a conference room inside. Then the camera pulls back to take in Haldin standing on a nearby balcony, as he looks in the window, takes careful aim at his target, and shoots him dead.

Allégret continues his emphasis on the visual by adroitly using a visual metaphor to begin the scene in which Razumov enters his darkened flat and sees someone lurking in the shadows. He strikes a match and recognizes Haldin; then he lights a lamp as his visitor volunteers that it is he who has assassinated the prime minister. The illumination that gradually fills the room implies the way that Haldin is gradually shedding light on his dark and murky plot. After Razumov hears his story, he leaves the exhausted Haldin to rest and goes out for a brief period.

When he returns, Razumov is terrified to find a police raid in progress in the building where he lives, since he fears that the police will find Haldin in his apartment. In his panic Razumov decides on the spur of the moment to go to the secret police and give up Haldin, before they discover Haldin in his flat and accuse him of harboring a fugitive. As it happens, the police are searching for someone else in the building, but Razumov does not know that.

After informing on Haldin, Razumov goes back to his lodgings, where Haldin is waiting to say goodbye.

Haldin says he regrets that he endangered Razumov and offers him his ring in gratitude, but Razumov declines to accept the gift. He does not want to possess anything belonging to Haldin that might link him to the fugitive. Later in the film Allégret will make significant use of Haldin's ring, when it returns to haunt Razumov. Haldin now clasps Razumov in a farewell embrace; but Razumov does not hug him back, although Haldin does not seem to notice. Razumov's passive reaction to Haldin's embrace offers further evidence of his implicit desire to distance himself from Haldin as far as possible. As he hears Haldin's footsteps retreating down the stairs, Razumov grabs at his overcoat collar and unbuttons it, as if he were suffocating. His gesture expresses visually the fact that he feels that he is being smothered by the anxiety and tension of being embroiled with a terrorist on the run.

In the novel Razumov has no misgivings about his betrayal of Haldin to the secret police, immediately after he turns him in. But in the film Razumov decides on an impulse to warn Haldin about his impending arrest, so that he can elude capture. He rushes out into the street, looking for Haldin, but stops in his tracks when he sees a gloved hand beckoning him from the window of a carriage that is parked by the curb. It is the chief of the secret police, who warns him that it is too late for him to try to interfere with the apprehension of Haldin.

Allégret now picks up on a symbolic image which Conrad employed in the book, and uses it to similar effect at this point in the film. Razumov goes back upstairs to his flat and looks at his pocket watch, apparently wondering if Haldin has been taken into custody as yet; then he nervously closes his hand over the watch. This image implies that Razumov is aware that time is running out for the anarchist, and his hour of doom is approaching.

In the film, as in the book, Razumov journeys to Geneva after Haldin is arrested and hanged, in order to spy on the members of the resistance group who were associates of Haldin's, at the behest of the Russian secret police. Ironically, Haldin's best friend Laspara, who is the ringleader of the group, assumes that Razumov was also a close friend of Haldin's as well; and, like Haldin's other comrades, he has no inkling that Razumov was instrumental in Haldin's capture.

During Razumov's first meeting with Laspara and the others, he happens to look up at a picture of Haldin hanging on the wall, which is festooned with flowers in loving memory of a deceased comrade. The picture is photographed in close-up to indicate how large it looms in Razumov's mind, for the image of Haldin is a painful reminder of Razumov's guilt. Razumov silently drops his eyes in dejection and shame at the sight of the photograph, but no one in the room notices.

When Razumov returns to his apartment on one occasion, he finds Haldin's ring lying on the mantel, waiting for him. It is a reminder, courtesy of the Russian secret police, that Razumov had a hand in Haldin's death, and that the police will reveal his betrayal of Haldin to Laspara's band, if he does not continue to spy on them. So Haldin's ring now serves as a threat to Razumov, and no longer as an emblem of Haldin's friendship for him. Razumov is so shocked by the sudden reappearance of the ring that he collapses into unconsciousness.

Razumov is at last overwhelmed by pangs of guilt for his betrayal of Haldin, of which Haldin's ring is a grim memento. As a result, he decides to confess his guilt to Laspara and the others. In the movie Nikita thereupon shoots Razumov dead in retaliation for his treachery—a punishment quite different from the one Razumov endures in the book.

The sequence which encompasses Razumov's confession and death is photographed and edited in a masterful way which indicates that Allégret is clearly in control of his material. Razumov meets Laspara on the staircase that leads to his apartment in the tenement where he lives. He makes his confession to Laspara there and then, and as he does so he collapses abjectly on the staircase. Razumov is photographed at this point through the bars of the banister railing, to indicate how Razumov is imprisoned by his guilt and shame. Laspara, horrified by Razumov's admission, turns his back on him and ascends the stairs to his apartment on the floor above, as Razumov grovels on the stairwell below him. In turning his back on Razumov, both literally and figuratively, Laspara implies how Razumov has made himself an outcast from the circle of Haldin's old friends and fellow anarchists. Razumov descends the stairs and goes out on the street; and Nikita follows him and shoots him in the back. As Razumov slips to the ground in death, he whispers to his executioner, "Merci, Nikita," and the film ends.

The confession scene just described is a fine example of the care and solid craftsmanship with which Allégret has invested his film adaptation of *Under Western Eyes*. Moreover, Pauline Kael rightly praises the director because he "doesn't try to soften the malevolent, tragic material."[8] Consequently, I warmly endorse film scholar Steve Vineberg's assessment of the film that *Razumov* is "worthy of inclusion in the catalogue of important Conrad films."[9]

The Secret Agent: The Novel

Conrad's other great novel about spies and terrorists is *The Secret Agent*, which was also filmed in 1936, the same year as *Razumov*. In his "Author's Note" to the novel in the Collected Edition Conrad explains in great detail the real-life models for the principal characters in the novel. "The subject of *The Secret Agent*," Conrad recalls, "came to me in the shape of a few words uttered by a friend [Ford Madox Ford] in a casual conversation about anarchists." As he and his companion passed on to the discussion of some episodes of terrorism, Conrad continues, they remembered an attempt to blow up the Greenwich Observatory in London on February 15, 1861, by one Martial Bourdin, who was blown to bits in his failed attempt to destroy the Observatory. "As to the outer wall," Conrad commented, "it did not show so much as the faintest crack."

As their conversation continued, Ford added, almost as an afterthought, "Oh, that fellow was half an idiot. His sister committed suicide."[10] In addition, it was thought that Bourdin, the mental retardate who was the actual perpetrator of the crime, was led on by his brother-in-law, H. B. Samuels, who was the editor of a notorious anarchist newspaper.

With these facts in mind, along with the aid of some additional material which Conrad drew from contemporary newspaper accounts of the Greenwich Observatory episode, he began to fashion the plot of *The Secret Agent*. In the book Bourdin became the mentally retarded Stevie; his sister became Stevie's sister Winnie Verloc; and Samuels, Bourdin's brother-in-law, became Stevie's brother-in-law, Mr. Verloc, the secret agent of the title. (As a matter of fact, the novel began its creative life as a short story which Conrad entitled "Verloc." But as the pages of the manuscript grew, he realized that he was developing a full-scale novel.)

Like *Under Western Eyes*, *The Secret Agent* takes place in the asphalt jungle of a big city. And London in the novel is portrayed, like Moscow in *Western Eyes*, as a grimy, hostile wilderness—little different from the jungles of Conrad's other works. It thus makes one wonder just how "civilized" modern society really is.

In the book Winnie weds Mr. Verloc, the proprietor of a softcore pornographic book shop, which masquerades as a stationery store. Although Verloc is several years her senior, she marries him in order to provide a secure home for her mentally retarded younger brother Stevie. Winnie is unaware that Verloc's disreputable occupation as a small-time pornographer is merely a front for his clandestine activities as an anarchist. He is really working secretly in London for an unidentified foreign power—though Conrad implies more than once that it is Russia. Inspector Heat, the chief adversary of Verloc and his band of terrorists, finds anarchists an inscrutable group to fathom. He prefers coping with burglars and thieves. "He could understand the mind of the burglar, because, as a matter of fact, the mind and instincts of a burglar are the same kind as the mind and instincts of a police officer. Both recognize the same conventions, and have a working knowledge of each other's methods and of the routine of their respective trade. They understand each other, which is advantageous to both, and establishes a sort of amenity in their relations."

On the other hand, "the mind of Inspector Heat was inaccessible to the ideas of revolt" (92). The revolutionary whom Heat finds it most difficult to understand is the one known only by the code name "the Professor," who supplies Verloc with explosives for his terrorist plots. The Professor is a true fanatic, one whose goal in life is the total destruction of the present social order because he believes that it has outlived its usefulness. In harmony with this ambition, the Professor is determined to create the perfect detonator with which to trigger his bombs, in order to fashion the most efficient instrument of destruction possible.

"The Professor's desire to destroy existing society in *The Secret Agent*," writes Jeremy Hawthorn, is "finally seen as negative and evil." Yet, Hawthorn continues, the Professor himself throughout the book sees his goal as reasonable; and, on this point, Hawthorn cites Conrad scholar Graham Holderness's paraphrase of the Professor's conviction that his goal is just: "What can be done with a world like this one, once it has been created; a world devoid of internal possibilities for redemption or improvement? There is only one final solution: destruction."[11]

The Professor vows that he will never be arrested because he carries with him at all times the means of his own self-destruction: a detonator hidden in his pocket, with which he can blow himself to kingdom come if he is cornered by the police. He sees a curious affinity between anarchists and policemen. "The terrorist and the policeman both come from the same basket," he muses. "Revolution, legality—counter moves in the same game" (69). He is convinced that the guardians of the law are quite as capable of violence, in their efforts to subdue the anarchists, as the anarchists are in carrying out their terrorist conspiracies. Indeed, nothing would please him more, says the Professor, than for the police to take to shooting the anarchists down in the streets in broad daylight; for that would mean that the police had become as brutal and violent as the terrorists themselves. According to the Professor, Gurko writes, "only by encouraging the defenders of law and order to embrace illegal and immoral means can the principle of legality and the system based upon it be undermined."[12] The Professor, possessed as he is by his singleminded dedication to violence and destruction, is one of the most fascinating characters in the novel.

Unknown to Winnie, Verloc gives Stevie a package containing a time bomb, supplied to him by the Professor. Verloc instructs Stevie to deposit the parcel at the Greenwich Observatory; and the hapless Stevie follows Verloc's instructions to the letter—except that he stumbles over a bush in the yard outside the Observatory, accidentally sets off the bomb prematurely, and is himself blown to fragments.

Stevie had always felt a sincere reverence for Verloc, for the fatherless lad implicitly saw Verloc as a father-figure. Similarly, Winnie Verloc viewed her husband as a surrogate father for Stevie. In fact, she had assured Verloc that the boy "would go through fire for you" (184); and, as Catharine Rising wryly remarks, Stevie finally did.

It was unfortunate that Winnie knew nothing of Verloc's nefarious profession as an anarchist, and that she furthermore was unaware that Verloc had involved her beloved brother in his activities. But she was simply living by her golden rule that "things do not stand much looking into"—a conviction based on the questionable assumption that what you don't know can't hurt you (177). Consequently, Winnie had never bothered to inquire into her husband's private life, and hence she only learned the truth about Verloc's covert activities after Stevie died in his futile effort to carry out one of Verloc's terrorist plots.

When Winnie finally discovers what happened to Stevie, she realizes with deep anguish that, as Rising puts it, "Verloc has ended her supreme illusion: that he and Stevie might be father and son."[13] Crazed with grief, Winnie wreaks revenge on Verloc for the death of her beloved brother by murdering him with a carving knife.

Film scholar Paul Kirschner points out in his essay on Conrad and film that one of Conrad's vividly imagined scenes could easily be transferred to the movie screen. In fact, Conrad himself noted that he could at times write in a style that was suitable for cinema. In recalling an abortive attempt which he and Stephen Crane made to collaborate on a play in the mid-1880s, he commented, "It occurs to me that Crane and I must have been unconsciously penetrated by a prophetic sense of the technique and of the very spirit of film plays, of which even the name was unknown then to the world."[14] As Kirschner mentions, the stabbing scene in *The Secret Agent* is a premier example of one of Conrad's vividly realized scenes, a scene that could therefore be transplanted virtually intact to the cinema.

As Conrad composed the episode in the novel, the carving knife is prominent from the beginning of the scene. "Mrs. Verloc's wifely forethought had left the cold beef on the table with carving knife and fork and half a loaf of bread for Mr. Verloc's supper" (231). Then Verloc is pictured employing the knife to carve the meat and cut the bread, as he devours his meal. When he is finished, Verloc lies down on the living room couch, and Winnie moves toward him with murder on her mind:

> She started forward at once. . . . Her right hand skimmed slightly the end of the table, and when she had passed on towards the sofa the carving knife had vanished without the slightest sound from the side of the dish. . . . He was lying on his back and staring upwards. He saw partly on the ceiling and partly on the wall the moving shadow of an arm with a clenched hand holding a carving knife. It fluttered up and down. . . . Mr. Verloc [had not] the time to move either hand or foot. The knife was already planted in his breast. . . . Mr. Verloc, the Secret Agent, turning slightly on his side with the force of the blow, expired without stirring a limb, in the muttered sound of the word 'Don't' by way of protest (262-63).

Kirschner sums up the scene by saying that, although Conrad had probably never seen a film when he wrote *The Secret Agent* in 1906, "a director would not be hard put to translate this sequence into terms of a shooting script."[15] Needless to say, Alfred Hitchcock modeled the stabbing scene in his film adaptation of *The Secret Agent* on Conrad's depiction of the episode in the novel.

After Winnie kills her husband, she flees the scene of the crime, determined to avoid being captured by the police and executed for her dark deed. And so—like Jones in *Victory*—she drowns herself rather than face prosecution for what she has done.

The Secret Agent: The Play

The Secret Agent: A Simple Tale received enough favorable notices to encourage Conrad to consider the possibility of dramatizing the story for the stage. Conrad prepared his stage version of the novel in late 1919 and early 1920, but he was not successful in finding a producer who was willing to mount a stage production in London's West End for another two years. Conrad's dramatization was finally produced on the London stage at the Ambassador Theater, where it ran for ten performances, beginning on November 2, 1922.

Conrad attended some of the rehearsals of the play, only to complain afterward, according to Roger Tennant, in his biography of Conrad, that he was nearly driven to distraction by the inability of the actors to interpret his meaning.

He could not bring himself to attend the opening night's performance, however, but spent the evening in the lounge of his hotel, nervously smoking cigarettes. The reviews of the opening night's performance were so disappointing that Conrad later claimed that the play, which he never saw in actual performance, "was put to death by the press."[16]

The only substantial departure that Conrad made in his dramatization of the original novel is that Winnie does not commit suicide at play's end as she does at the end of the book. Nevertheless, as William Houze observes in his unpublished thesis about the play, in the wake of her savage murder of her husband and the loss of her beloved brother, she is "shown to be totally destroyed in mind and spirit"; indeed, as the curtain falls, the onlookers "can only stare dumbly at the spectacle of Winnie's destruction."[17]

As a matter of fact, Conrad feared, even while he was working on the play, that the theater audiences of his day might find his tale of madness and despair a rather sordid and shocking enterprise. When he was writing the second act in November, 1919, he confided to Pinker, his agent, "To make an audience of comfortable, easy-going people sup on horrors in a hopeless enterprise."[18] Perhaps the grim storyline of the play, epitomized in its bleak denouement, helps to account for the failure of the drama to gain favor with theater audiences. Conrad biographer John Batchelor adds that another reason that the play failed was that Conrad was simply not sufficiently skilled as a playwright to do justice to the novel in his stage dramatization.[19]

At all events, although Conrad was never much taken with the silent pictures of his time, he did speculate at one point whether or not this particular novel might make a better movie than a play, since he had found it very difficult to confine the story's action with the limitations imposed by the proscenium arch of the conventional theater. Alfred Hitchcock, for one, saw the cinematic possibilities in the novel, and in due course brought it to the screen.

Sabotage: The Film

In his Foreword to this book, "Fiction versus Film," Graham Greene, usually Hitchcock's nemesis among commentators on British cinema, wrote with guarded approval that Hitchcock's 1936 film version of Conrad's *The Secret Agent* preserved at least some of what Greene termed the ruthlessness of the classic novel from which it was derived. Hitchcock generally shied away from using the revered works of major writers as his sources for film subjects, because critics too often expected the film version of literary works to be too rigidly faithful to the originals.

In choosing to film Conrad's 1907 book, however, Hitchcock was really not breaking his rule, because Conrad's works in general—and certainly this novel in particular—had not as yet attained the prestigious critical status they would come to enjoy later on. (As a matter of fact, *The Secret Agent* received only mixed reviews when it was published.) Hence the novel was not considered to be any more sacrosanct a literary source for a movie than Somerset Maugham's volume of short stories about secret agent Richard Ashenden, which Hitchcock had filmed the same year under the title *Secret Agent*.

In addition, Conrad's novel was a suspenseful tale of international intrigue. This was a subject that was naturally tempting to the director; and Conrad's austere Catholic vision of man as God made him, adrift in a hostile, barbaric world, that God never made, most likely appealed to Hitchcock's own Catholic sensibilities as well.

The first alteration in the novel which Hitchcock made in adapting it for film was to change the title. This was a practical necessity since, as noted earlier, Hitchcock's previous film, which he derived from Maugham's *Ashenden* stories, was entitled *Secret Agent* (often incorrectly referred to as *The Secret Agent*). Accordingly, Hitchcock entitled his film version of Conrad's *The Secret Agent* (with attendant confusion of titles) *Sabotage*. Frederick Karl has compounded the confusion by baldly stating in his Conrad biography that no less than three films have been derived from Conrad's novel: *The* [sic] *Woman Alone*, *Sabotage*, and *I Married a Murderer*.[20] To set the record straight, *A Woman Alone* is merely the title under which *Sabotage* was initially released in the United States; and *I Married a Murderer* is simply not the name of any existing film—whether based on Conrad's novel or anything else.

Earl G. Ingersoll gives a handy list of examples of the changes that Hitchcock made in the plot and setting of Conrad's novel in order to create his film version of the book. The list includes the following:

'For example, Hitchcock changed the time setting from the 1880's to the 1920's, and discarded many of the minor characters,' Ingersoll observes. Thus Hitchcock's Stevie is a younger and brighter child than the twenty-year-old Stevie of the novel, who is, as we know, a mental retardate. 'And Mrs. Verloc, played by thirties star Sylvia Sidney, is made pretty enough to attract the attention of a young and handsome police officer named Ted (John Loder),' in order to provide some love interest for the movie—since it is painfully obvious that Mrs. Verloc (who inexplicably has no first name in the film, though she is called Winnie in the book) does not love her husband.[21] The novel's Inspector Heat 'disappears into the new character Ted,' to use Anderegg's phrase, in order to provide the film with some romantic interest, as already noted.[22]

In Hitchcock's updated movie adaptation, Mr. Verloc (Oscar Homolka), a down-at-the-heels middle-European, operates a seedy flea-ridden cinema in East London, instead of the combination stationery/pornography shop he owns in the book. In any event, his business is but a front for his subversive activities on behalf of an unnamed foreign power, although actor Homolka's bona fide German accent suggests that the country in question is Nazi Germany. The implication of Nazi intrigue in England is also suggested by the accents of the German spies in Hitchcock's *The Man Who Knew Too Much* (1934) and his *39 Steps* (1935).

The movie opens with a printed dictionary definition of sabotage which then serves as a background for the credits: "Willful destruction of buildings or machinery, with the object of alarming a group of persons or inspiring public uneasiness."

The film proper begins with a close-up of a burning light bulb, followed by a shot of a brightly lit London thoroughfare. Then there is a shot of the same light bulb flickering and going out, followed by a shot of the same street plunged into darkness. There has been a power failure, and we next see workmen in a power plant discovering that a saboteur has put sand in the machinery to cause the breakdown. One of the workmen asks the other, "Who did it?" His question is answered for the audience as the camera cuts to the saboteur in question, Mr. Verloc, as he sneaks home to the family apartment, which is behind the cinema he operates. As he washes his hands, some telltale silt from his hands swirls down the drain: it is some of the sand which the workmen in the power plant found in the machinery. He then lies down, pretending to sleep. When his wife enters the bedroom, he tells her he has been home all evening. In this remarkably economical opening sequence Hitchcock lets the audience know that Verloc is a saboteur and that his wife is not aware of his subversive operations. These activities include perpetrating incidents like the blackout, which are calculated to spread mass hysteria throughout London, in order to distract the British government from events that are taking place abroad.

After the blackout incident, Verloc's superior orders him to dynamite the subway station in Piccadilly Circus. Verloc receives his orders during a secret meeting with his employer in the aquarium at the zoo, while they are ostensibly looking at a tank full of sea creatures. As Donald Spoto describes the scene, Verloc is told "to plant a bomb in Piccadilly Circus on Saturday, the Lord Mayor's Show Day." Verloc protests that he does not want to be responsible for the loss of human life, but then he weakens and accepts the assignment. "Left alone to contemplate the deadly effect of his task, Verloc gazes at a rectangular fish tank, and from his point of view we see the swimming fish."

Then Verloc fantasizes that he sees a vision of Piccadilly Circus inside the tank. He further imagines that he sees an explosion which causes the buildings first to sway and then to get sucked down the drain, as if someone had pulled the plug in the tank. "Finally, the image redissolves back to the peacefully swimming fish." Spoto concludes that "water, archetypally, is the source of life and also of primal chaos."[23] Hence Hitchcock in this scene implicitly associates water with the chaos that Verloc is to cause with the act of sabotage he is to commit.

Anderegg astutely observes that this fantasy sequence was suggested by one of Conrad's descriptions of London in the novel as murky, gloomy, and damp. More precisely, when Conrad pictures the Assistant Commissioner of Police leaving his office at one point, he writes that, when the man descended into the street, his descent was like "the descent into a slimy aquarium from which the water had been run off" (147). Anderegg comments that the fantasy scene in the film is effective in bringing to life Conrad's dark view of London in the novel, "as well as indicating the guilty apprehension and fear that will dominate Verloc" as he sets about implementing his grim task.[24]

Verloc is supplied with bombs made to order by the Professor (William Dewhurst), the harmless-looking owner of a pet shop. Greene thought Dewhurst was superb as "a soapy old scoundrel who supports his shrewish daughter and her bastard child with a bird business, concocting his explosives in the one living room among the child's dolls and the mother's washing." (By contrast, the Professor is a loner with no family in the book.)

A major change that Hitchcock made in his film of Conrad's book is the portrayal on the screen of the explosion in which Stevie is killed, rather than having it take place "off stage" as it does in both the book and play, where it is reported in a newspaper account.

Verloc entrusts his wife's younger brother Stevie (Desmond Tester) with the task of delivering an ordinary-looking parcel to the men's room at Piccadilly Circus subway station, on the way to return a film ominously entitled *Bartholomew the Strangler* to Verloc's distributor. The package in fact contains a time bomb set to go off at 1:45 P.M. As luck would have it, the well-meaning but inept youngster is delayed by the congestion surrounding the Lord Mayor's Day parade, and decides to take a bus the rest of the distance to make up for lost time. The affable bus conductor at first hesitates to let the boy on board carrying motion-picture film, which in those days contained combustible nitrate; but he finally gives in to the lad's pleading.

It is not the cans of celluloid, ironically enough, but Stevie's other package that should have been the conductor's chief concern; it is that which explodes before Stevie can reach his destination, killing himself and the whole busload of innocent people. Hitchcock often said that portraying this lovable, freckle-faced boy perishing in such a dreadful fashion was a cardinal sin, since it elicited a severely negative audience response. In the novel, the young man likewise dies in an explosion, but Conrad was careful not to engage the reader's sympathy for Stevie to the same degree as Hitchcock does in the film. Conrad's Stevie is not an awkward adolescent, but a mental retardate who remains a remote figure, and hence the reader never really gets to know him, much less become involved with him.

Besides, as we are aware, the disaster takes place "off stage" in the book, where it is reported after the fact, thus keeping the boy's personal fate from absorbing the reader's attention more than his subsidiary function in the story would warrant. For Conrad, in short, Stevie is more of a plot device than a person, since his death drives Mrs. Verloc to wreak vengeance on her husband at the climax of the story.

On reflection, Hitchcock thought that at the very least he should have followed Conrad's lead by having Stevie's demise occur off screen. His reasoning was that when a director stages a suspenseful incident of this kind, usually the audience implicitly assumes that he does so for no other purpose than to show the helpless person who is endangered being saved in the nick of time, thus relieving the tension that he has built up. The audience consequently feels cheated if the threatened peril actually overtakes the innocent party, and they are therefore denied the satisfaction of seeing the individual emerge unharmed. In depicting the gruesome bus calamity as he does, Hitchcock is rather like the director of an old silent serial showing the heroine who is tied to the railroad track really being run over by an oncoming train!

In fact, when I spoke with Hitchcock, he recalled that after the London press screening of *Sabotage* the female critic of *The London Observer* came up to him with raised fists and shouted, "How dare you do a thing like that! I've got a five-year-old son at home!" Interestingly enough, by the time Hitchcock made *Psycho* (1960) he could dispatch a sympathetic character (the leading lady) right before the eyes of the audience as he did Stevie in *Sabotage* without protests, since by then the public had learned to expect the unexpected from his films.

In any event, after Stevie is dead, Hitchcock prefaces the sequence in which Mrs. Verloc murders her husband to avenge her brother's death with a brief scene in which she wanders in a benumbed state through the cinema on her way back to the Verloc quarters behind it. On the screen is a Walt Disney cartoon in which an unidentified bird shoots a robin with an arrow, and a bass voice intones on the sound track the old ditty "Who Killed Cock Robin?" Mrs. Verloc winces, for she knows who killed Stevie. "It is a short step," Anderegg writes, "from an arrow to a carving knife."[25]

This scene is followed shortly afterwards by the stabbing scene, which is superbly shot and edited. While carving a roast at the dinner table, Mrs. Verloc finds herself contemplating Stevie's useless death. The camera gives us a series of close-ups: of Stevie's model sailboat and his bird cage, plus his empty chair at the table—all of which serve as mute reminders of the absent boy. The two caged parakeets, moreover, suggest Mrs. Verloc's horrible realization that, without being aware of it, both she and Stevie had been imprisoned like captive canaries with a man who, unbeknownst to them, has been engaged in dangerous undercover work that could well have resulted in some catastrophe long before this.

Close-ups of Mrs. Verloc's tormented face, and of her hand grasping the carving knife to slice the meat and scoop vegetables onto her husband's plate, are intercut with shots of his watching apprehensively, sensing that she is unconsciously forming an inner resolve to turn the knife on him. As Hitchcock himself describes the scene, "The camera cuts from her hand to her eyes"; then to Verloc; "then back to the hand holding the knife." Next "the camera moves again to Verloc—back to the knife—back again to his face. You see him seeing the knife, realizing its implications."[26] Verloc lunges for the instrument; but he struggles with his wife in such an ineffectual way that one can only assume that he is accepting his death as justly imposed by her, as the knife is plunged into his stomach like the arrow that found its mark in Cock Robin. Spoto comments that Verloc seems to walk into the knife; to kill himself.[27]

The present scene is a clear-cut example of Hitchcock's conviction, expressed in his 1937 essay on direction, that "the screen ought to speak its own language, freshly coined, and it can't do that unless it treats an acted scene as a piece of raw material which . . . can be woven into an expressive visual pattern." Specifically, the filmgoer is much more involved in a scene that is broken up into a series of individual shots taken at close range, than by one recorded from some distance away in a single static take, as if it were "a long piece of stage acting." Using the camera to focus on each significant detail, he contended, enables the director "to draw the audience right inside the situation instead of leaving them to watch it from outside," as if they were at a play rather than a film.[28]

The stabbing scene in the film pretty much follows the scene in the book, described in detail earlier, except that in the novel there is no question of Verloc acquiescing in his death. He is completely surprised by Winnie's murderous intent, and does not have time to defend himself adequately against her onslaught. By contrast, Hitchcock made it appear in the film that Verloc virtually committed suicide by not putting up more of a struggle to avoid the fatal knife blade. The director's reason for filming the scene this way was that he feared the audience would not sympathize with the heroine if she turned out to be a cold-blooded murderess.

Sylvia Sidney was initially upset by Hitchcock's insistence that she play this scene without recourse to dialogue. But Hitchcock, who never lost his predilection, dating back to the silent era, for stressing the visual elements of cinema over the verbal, assured her that she could convey wordlessly the emotions called for by the tense situation. She could and did.

The Professor subsequently goes to Verloc's apartment and is stunned to discover Verloc's corpse. Moreover, he realizes that the police are closing in on the building, with a view to arresting Verloc for sabotage. Fearing that he will be accused of the murder by the police, the Professor detonates the bomb he is carrying with him and thereby commits suicide by blowing up the building. Thus in the film the Professor destroys himself with one of his own bombs—something, we recall, he threatened to do more than once in the novel, but never did. The police assume, of course, that Verloc was killed in the blast, and hence there is no evidence, as far as they are concerned, to incriminate Mrs. Verloc in her husband's death.

Although Hitchcock eschews Conrad's conclusion to the story, in which Winnie Verloc drowns herself in despair after killing her husband, the ending he substitutes is still fairly bleak and very much in keeping with Winnie Verloc's oft-repeated observation in the book that things do not stand much looking into; that is, the unspoken motivations that frequently underlie people's behavior generally will not survive close scrutiny. In this instance, Ted successfully blocks Mrs. Verloc's attempt to confess to the police that she knifed her husband accidentally-on-purpose during a scuffle at the dinner table. He does so, not particularly because of his conviction that the anarchist got his just deserts, but because of his own ripening love for Verloc's widow. The film thus ends with Mrs. Verloc and Ted both ruefully aware that, for all practical purposes, he is helping her get away with murder; and that their punishment will be to live with that realization for the rest of their days.

In sum, the liberties that Hitchcock took with his source story in bringing Conrad's *Secret Agent* to the screen are in keeping with the spirit of the novel. Hence, like *Razumov*, made the same year, it deserves a prominent place among the better screen versions of Conrad's work.

Nevertheless, Hitchcock's film version of *The Secret Agent* was accorded a less-than-enthusiastic reception by the mass audience when it was released. It seems, then, that film audiences at the time were no more prepared to accept the dark and gruesome events which Conrad's story depicted than theater audiences had been when his stage version of the novel was produced earlier. Nevertheless, the film over the years has gained a well-deserved reputation as a vintage Hitchcock thriller.

Chapter 4

Paradise Lost:
An Outcast of the Islands (1952)

An Outcast of the Islands: The Novel

In turning to *An Outcast of the Islands,* it is appropriate to point out that Conrad wrote three novels that are interrelated because some of the same characters appear in all three. For example, Captain Tom Lingard appears in *Almayer's Folly* (1895), *An Outcast of the Islands* (1896), and *The Rescue* (1920). Consequently the three novels, taken together, comprise what Karl calls in *A Reader's Guide to Conrad* a trilogy in reverse. This is because *Almayer's Folly,* though written first, is set at a time when Lingard is an elderly man; *Outcast* takes place when Lingard is in middle life; and *The Rescue* is set when Lingard is still a dashing young mariner—young enough, as we have seen, to have a torrid love affair with Edith Travers.

Tom Lingard, as mentioned, was modeled on Captain William Lingard, a successful European trader who lived and worked in the tropics. By the same token, Willems, the title character of *Outcast of the Islands,* was modeled on a man that Conrad once met while on a voyage in the tropics. Conrad had dinner one evening in an Eastern port with a Dutch trader named Charlie Olmeyer who, as we shall shortly see, inspired the character of Kaspar Almayer (Conrad's Anglicized version of the Dutchman's last name) in *Almayer's Folly* and *Outcast of the Islands.*

As Conrad recalls in his "Author's Note" to *Outcast* in the Collected Edition, the man who was to serve as the inspiration for Peter Willems in *Outcast* was present at the dinner table, but he was largely ignored by the other diners. His career as a trader in the tropics had been an abysmal failure, and the other Europeans kept their distance from him, as if his failure was somehow contagious. Conrad remembers that "the man who suggested Willems to me"—an alcoholic Hollander named Carl de Veer—"was not particularly interesting in himself. My interest was aroused by his dependent status . . . as a disliked, worn-out European, living on the reluctant toleration of [the] Settlement." Conrad continues by saying that during the daylight hours this hopeless alcoholic could be seen wandering silently among the houses of the Settlement, "almost as dumb as any animal and apparently much more homeless. I don't know what he did with himself at night." Conrad goes on to say that the evening he dined with Olmeyer, "there was Willems sitting at the table with us like the skeleton at the feast, obviously shunned by everyone, never addressed by anyone."[1]

As noted before, Almayer himself was suggested to Conrad by Charles Olmeyer, who had a long career as a trader in the tropics. Conrad recalls in *A Personal Record* that the first time he ever set eyes on Olmeyer, the latter was standing on a pier nearby where Conrad's own ship was docked. Conrad says that he had heard of Olmeyer in Singapore and also aboard his own ship when the passengers were gossiping about the locals. And so Charles Olmeyer became, without ever knowing it, Conrad's Kaspar Almayer in both *Almayer's Folly* and *An Outcast of the Islands.*[2]

In *Almayer's Folly* and its companion piece, *An Outcast of the Islands,* both Almayer and Willems are portrayed as protegés of Tom Lingard, since Lingard has helped both of them get started in the trading business in the tropical ports of the Malay Archipelago, where the two men live and work. In *Outcast* Lingard arranges employment for Willems as a clerk in a trading company in Macassar. Willems solidifies his position in the firm by marrying Joanna, the half-caste daughter of Huldig, his employer. His wife's poor relatives are a constant drain on Willems's finances, however; and he eventually begins embezzling money from the company in order to meet their demands, so that they will maintain their admiration of him as a prestigious, prosperous white business man.

Willems sees his manipulation of the firm's funds as a temporary expedient. As Conrad describes Willems's attitude toward his dishonest activities, "When he stepped off the straight and narrow path of . . . honesty, it was with an inward assertion of unflinching resolve to fall back again into the monotonous but safe stride of virtue, as soon as his little excursion into the wayside quagmires" had served its purpose (p. 3).

Commenting on this passage, Heliéna Krenn opines that "Peter Willems is introduced as a young man who lacks moral fibre. He is devoid of any sense of spiritual or social values beyond those that gratify his vanity, and with great consistency he refuses to assume responsibility for his conduct."[3] An index of Willems's questionable moral principles is his insistence that it is not wrong to embezzle funds from the firm as long as he fully intends to pay back what he has misappropriated for his private use.

As a matter of fact, Willems is in the process of paying back the money he has taken from the company's coffers when Huldig discovers what he has been up to and promptly dismisses him. Needless to say, Willems has trouble finding another position elsewhere in Macassar because of his patent dishonesty; and in this manner he becomes the outcast of the novel's title. With Lingard's help, Willems endeavors to get a fresh start in life, and moves on to Lingard's trading post in the remote port of Sambir, where Almayer is also stationed. Willems's wife Joanna, for her part, rejects her husband as a criminal, and consequently refuses to accompany him to Sambir, but stays behind instead in Macassar.

As the story unfolds, the isolation of Willems's jungle surroundings causes him to become restless and bored, and he therefore easily succumbs to the charms of the sultry Malayan native girl Aïssa. "In the character of Aïssa," Ruth Nadelhaft observes, "Conrad has created a woman of enormous charm and beauty who attracts and terrifies" Willems. In fact, "Aïssa's effect upon Willems from the first is captivating."[4]

Stephen Land goes so far as to say that Willems's infatuation with Aïssa takes on the character of demonic possession.[5] Thus, in one scene in the novel, Conrad depicts Aïssa's seductive gaze as enchanting Willems: "With that look she drew the man's soul away from him," and engendered in him "an ecstasy of the senses," which took total possession of him. "He never stirred a limb, hardly breathed, but stood in stiff immobility, absorbing the delight of her close contact by every pore" (140).

Although he views himself with considerable self-contempt, the slave of passion, Willems cannot extricate himself from his sexual entanglement with this wild creature of the jungle, and ultimately opts to marry her. But her Malayan tribesmen advise Willems that the only way they will allow him to marry into their tribe is on the condition that he will disclose to them the secret channel which leads from the ocean into Sambir. Because Lingard alone knows the secret river route into Sambir, he has enjoyed the highly lucrative privilege of exclusive trading rights with the natives of Sambir up to now. The native tribesmen want to break his trade monopoly, therefore, in order to allow them to deal with other trading companies as well.

Lingard has shared his trade secret about the channel route into Sambir only with his protegé Willems. Because of his infatuation with Aïssa, Willems eventually relents and reveals to the tribesmen how to navigate the access route into Sambir. Aïssa's tribe accordingly permits Willems to marry her; but since the Malayan chieftains have no further use for him, they decline to accept him into their society; and so Willems remains an outcast.

When Lingard discovers what Willems has done, he has a harrowing confrontation with him. Lingard angrily informs Willems in no uncertain terms that he has disowned him, both as a business associate and as a friend, in the light of Willem's betrayal of his trust. Willems begs Lingard for the chance to start over again, and promises that he will make good this time. Lingard replies bitterly:

"No promise of yours is any good to me. . . . You are my prisoner. You shall stay here. . . . You are not fit to go amongst people. . . . You are my mistake. I shall hide you here. If I let you go out you will go amongst unsuspecting men, and lie, and steal, and cheat. . . . Do not expect me to forgive you. To forgive you one must have been angry and become contemptuous, and there is nothing in me now—no anger, no contempt, no disappointment. To me you are not Willems the man I befriended and helped through thick and thin, and thought much of. . . . .You are my shame."

"You are alone," Lingard concludes. "Nothing can help you. Nobody will. You are neither white nor brown. You have no color as you have no heart. . . . You are buried here" (275-76). In these chilling words Lingard labels Willems as a perpetual outcast, a man who belongs nowhere. He has, in summary, written Willems off as a total loss and left him to his own devices. Furthermore, Lingard wishes to bury Willems in this remote part of the islands, not only as a punishment for Willems's treachery, but also because he does not wish the world at large to know how gullible he was in foolishly trusting such an unworthy and ungrateful creature.

Krenn comments at this point that, while Lingard is convinced that he is dealing fairly with his one-time protegé and is "meting out nothing but justice," he speaks of Willems as his shame. Thereby he admits that, in hiding away the man who has been the cause of his pride for many years, he disowns his mistake; he lowers himself to the level of Willems who consistently disowns his misdeeds, "and what Lingard calls an act of justice discloses itself as a primitive act of self-deceit. Lingard's behavior is prompted by the need to redeem his seriously shaken faith in himself."[6]

After Lingard finishes his condemnation of Willems, a storm erupts, accompanied by flashes of lighting and bursts of thunder. "The voice of thunder was heard, speaking in a sustained, emphatic and vibrant roll," Conrad writes, "with violent louder bursts of crashing sound, like a wrathful and threatening discourse of an angry god" (283). It is as it some deity were passing a thundering judgment on Willems to reinforce Lingard's own denunciation of his former protegé. The scene between Lingard and Willems just described, by the way, will turn up nearly intact in Reed's film of the novel.

Shortly after his confrontation with Lingard, Willems decides to be reunited with his first wife, Joanna, when she arrives in Sambir, seeking reconciliation with him. With her, he hopes to make a fresh start, this time in "the world he has deserted," says

Stephen Land; "the world of their marriage, his business con-
nections, and white respectability."[7]

Despite the author's earlier portrayal of Joanna as an
unattractive, unintelligent woman, adds Krenn, Conrad "gives
her role an unexpected turn when she becomes the potential
deliverer of her husband from captivity." Indeed, "she sum-
mons the courage and moral strength . . . to dare life with him
once more."[8]

Willems introduces Joanna to Aïssa as "my wife according to
our white law, which comes from God!" (355) Willems thus
invokes the law of God in order to endorse his marriage to
Joanna as a genuine Christian marriage, and thereby repudiate
his marriage to Aïssa. He does so, not because he has
developed religious scruples that his marriage to a pagan is
invalid, but because it now suits his purposes to shed Aïssa in
favor of returning to Joanna. By doing so, he demonstrates
once and for all what a rank opportunist he has been all along.
Joanna has brought along the little boy who is the offspring of
her marriage to Willems; and Aïssa is deeply chagrined to learn
that Willems and Joanna have a child, since she is aware that
the lad gives Joanna a hold on Willems which she does not
have.

Realizing that Aïssa is in a towering rage about the prospect
of losing Willems to Joanna, Willems whispers to Joanna to take
his gun and their son, run to the boat which she came in, and
wait for him there. Joanna rushes off with the child to the shore
without, however, taking the gun along; Aïssa swiftly grabs the
weapon instead. Crazed with sexual jealousy, Aïssa equivalently
tells Willems that if she cannot have him, no one else will
either. With that, she summarily shoots him dead, and the novel
draws to its tragic close.

An Outcast of the Islands: The Film

It was Ralph Richardson, who plays Lingard in the film, that
first interested Reed in Conrad's *Outcast of the Islands*. Reed
recalls that "while I was working on *The Fallen Idol* (1948),
Ralph Richardson asked me if I had ever read *Outcast*. I thought
I knew all of Conrad's books, but I had never read that one.

Immediately after I did, I fell in love with it and asked Ralph to play the captain."[9]

Reed's film adaptation of *Outcast* follows the plot of the novel very closely. The movie opens with the sequence in which Willems (Trevor Howard) is exposed as an embezzler and discharged by Huldig, his employer. The film then portrays Willems's arrival at the trading post in Sambir, where Lingard has arranged for him to work with Almayer. But instead of redeeming himself for his past indiscretions, Willems sinks ever deeper into moral degradation, epitomized by his mad passion for the alluring Malayan girl Aïssa (played by the Pakistani actress Kerima).

Willems and Aïssa do not share a common language in the film, as they do in the book, and hence cannot communicate with each other in words. Therefore, the native girl, in her silence, comes across as an inscrutable, intriguing goddess; and she is all the more fascinating to Willems for that reason. In his definitive study of Reed, Robert Moss describes Aïssa as a "dark-eyed beauty who moves about with regal but savage pride and communicates great emotional intensity. As the agent of Willems's downfall, she is completely persuasive."[10]

Reed portrays the development of Willems's sexual obsession for Aïssa very skillfully. Willems is mesmerized by her the first time he sits on the beach and observes her doing her daily chores. That night he lies awake in bed, enmeshed in the mosquito net that hangs over his bed—an apt metaphor for the manner in which Willems is becoming entangled in Aïssa's seductive charms.

One evening Almayer's wife (Wendy Hiller), who knows that Willems has been spending time with Aïssa, warns Willems against getting involved with the hypnotic temptress. "Are you afraid of what she is and what you might become? You would do well to be afraid." But Willems fails to heed Mrs. Almayer's entreaty. Later that same evening he asks Almayer (Robert Morley) with studied casualness if he can borrow a gun, on the pretext that he wants to hunt some deer. But Almayer is not taken in by his subterfuge. "What deer! It's a gazelle you're after," he retorts with undisguised contempt. "You want gold anklets and silk sarongs for that game, my mighty hunter." Undaunted,

Willems goes off in his rowboat to Aïssa's village to find her. Mrs. Almayer infers that he has finally consummated his affair with Aïssa when she notices the next morning that Willems's bed had not been slept in the previous night.

Reed portrays Willems as initially being loath to divulge Lingard's secret river route into Sambir when the leaders of Aïssa's tribe attempt to induce him to do so. In following this course the director creates suspense by making the viewer wonder whether or not Willems can maintain what is left of his honor by declining to betray Lingard. When Babalatchi, one of the tribal leaders (George Coulouris), coyly suggests that Willems reveal the river route, Willems storms out of the room, exclaiming, "Babalatchi, have you no sense of honor? No!"

Babalatchi then steps up his campaign to break down Willems's resistance to disclosing Lingard's navigational secret to the tribe by slyly intimating to Willems that this revelation is the price of his maintaining his relationship with Aïssa; but Willems still does not relent. On another occasion Babalatchi and his cohorts craftily imply that if Willems does their bidding, they will try to obtain a partnership for him in the new trading company that will be using Lingard's trade route, once it is made available to them.

The distraught Willems goes to Almayer, looking for some compassion and understanding in his plight. Willems implies that if Almayer were to raise his status at the trading post from that of a mere clerk to that of a full-fledged partner, he would not be so tempted to sell out Lingard to Babalatchi's faction, in order to obtain a partnership with the new trading company.

Almayer merely scoffs at Willems, indicating that he deserves no more authority at Lingard's trading post then Almayer has granted him. He dismisses Willems, saying, "You have thrown yourself on a savage woman who will kill you with her love or with her hate." Reed implies that Willems's venomous rejection by Almayer—coupled, needless to say, with Willems's desire to hold on to Aïssa—finally drives Willems to betray Lingard to the tribal leaders. As it happens, Lingard is away from Sambir during this period, and so he does not learn of Willems's treachery for some time.

Carol Reed's film version of *An Outcast of the Islands* is generally regarded by commentators on the Conrad films as one of
the most faithful adaptations of a Conrad story ever done on
film. And there is ample reason for agreeing with this critical
verdict on the movie. As an index of Reed's fidelity to the spirit
of his literary source, one need only point out how the director,
along with his collaborator, screenwriter William Fairchild, is at
pains to transfer into the movie several major scenes from the
novel.

For example, Reed brings over into the film the powerful
sequence which follows Willems's disclosure of the secret trade
route to the natives. In this scene Willems leads a group of the
inhabitants of Sambir to Lingard's trading post. He gleefully
goads them to turn on Almayer, whom he despises for rejecting
him in the past, and sew him up in his own hammock and then
toss him in the air like a football. The filmgoer is aware, as he
watches Almayer's degradation graphically visualized on the
screen, that ever since Willems's involvement with Aïssa
became known, Almayer has lost no opportunity to denounce
Willems as a lecher and a lazy lout. In fact, Almayer had previously taught his young daughter Nina to taunt and tease
Willems by calling him a pig. Hence, during the present scene,
there is a shot of Nina, who apparently thinks she is at a party,
playfully calling her father a pig as he swings to and fro in the
hammock. As for the shots of Almayer himself, Moss comments
that, "with his weak chin and bulging eyes, he looks like an
astonished, terrified guppy."

Still, given Almayer's cruel treatment of Willems in the past,
the filmgoer is aware at this point that Almayer to that extent
deserves his comeuppance. Thus Moss concludes, "When
Willems leads the natives in the vengeful pillage of Almayer's
house, we enjoy his humiliation in the hammock."[11] Marcia
Landy no doubt had this scene in mind when she said of the
film, "The world portrayed in the film, particularly through the
character of Almayer, is violent and destructive."[12]

Reed has been careful to transcribe into his film some of the
most telling visual imagery from the book. Thus, after Lingard
returns to Sambir and discovers Willems's skullduggery, he
ponders how Willems has ruined his dreams of accruing a for-

tune in Sambir. As he does so, he is absentmindedly building a house of cards on a card table. Lingard contends that he is not licked yet, and that he will rebuild his private empire in Sambir. When the house of cards suddenly collapses on the table, however, it signals that Lingard's empty dream of wealth has collapsed like a house of cards.

Near the end of the film there is another major scene which has been taken over intact from the book to the film. By this time the Malayan tribesmen have banished Willems from their midst, once he is of no further use to them. Lingard journeys in a canoe to Willems's remote up-river camp, where Willems now lives with Aïssa, for a confrontation with him over the latter's betrayal of his business interests.

Wallace Watson comments that, as Lingard arrives in a canoe, there is a long shot of him "sitting straight and stiff as his simple seaman's code, which has been so violated by Willems."[13] The latter looks mangy and dissheveled as he meets Lingard. His shabby clothes are an ironic contrast to the immaculate business suits he once wore while in Huldig's employ. Indeed, the shots of Willem's wearing tattered rags suggest how his clothes have come to represent the last shreds of the respectability which he once displayed so proudly. With Aïssa by his side, Willems tries to make a show of defiance toward Lingard; but the latter merely slaps him, in a visual display of contempt for him. Willems cries, "I could have shot you!" "You would have missed," responds Lingard; "there is such a things as justice on this earth!"

In this scene Reed and Fairchild make use of Conrad's dialogue, as they do elsewhere in the film. For example, Lingard denounces Willems for his disloyalty in a lengthy speech taken *verbatim* from the book, which I have reproduced in part earlier in this chapter. He concludes with biting contempt, "You say you did this for her. Well, you have her!" Aïssa, smouldering with fury, wants Willems to avenge himself on Lingard for humiliating him; accordingly, there is a shot of her extending her hand toward Willems with his gun in it, wordlessly urging him to make good his earlier threat to shoot Lingard. Willems waves his gun at Lingard ominously as he cries out, "Don't provoke me, Capt. Lingard!" But Lingard merely sneers at him in

return: "Provoke you! What is there in you to provoke?" Finally
Willems shouts at Lingard in a threatening tone, "We shall
meet again, Capt. Lingard!" Lingard, in turn, does not bother
to answer.

The scene concludes with another example of visual imagery
that Reed has incorporated into the film from the book. After
finishing with Willems, Lingard gets into his canoe and orders
the native crew to take him home. We see Lingard get into the
canoe in long shot: he turns his back on Willems both literally
and figuratively (in much the same in which Lespara turns his
back on Razumov at the climax of *Razumov*), in order to serve
notice to Willems once and for all that he has written him off
for good, and will have nothing further to do with him.

The scene just described, which includes not only Lingard's
extended tirade at Willems, but also their seemingly endless
mutual recriminations, goes on too long. The patriarchal Lingard, after all, is simply too longwinded in his berating of
Willems, and eventually the viewer can find the scene
somewhat tedious. In my recent essay on Reed I quote him as
saying that he was prepared to concede this point to some
degree. "It's a funny thing," he told me; "a scene can be good at
three minutes; if it's overwritten into four, the extra minute
weakens it. On the other hand, a ten-minute scene may not be
too long if there is material enough in it to develop it for ten
minutes."[14]

In any event, in the wake of Lingard's departure, Willems,
along with Aïssa, who has witnessed the bitter quarrel between
the two men, returns to their hut, just as a tropical downpour
begins. Aïssa has become progressively more disillusioned with
Willems, the deeper he has sunk into degradation throughout
the course of the story. She is obviously appalled at the manner
in which the weak-willed Willems allowed Lingard to demean
and ridicule him; and hence she is at last thoroughly disgusted
with him. Thus Reed concludes the film with Lingard consign-
ing Willems to oblivion with a woman who is utterly estranged
from him. As Watson describes the concluding shot of the
movie, Willems is "peering out of his hut while Aïssa sits at the
door disgusted at his weakness but still poised, tragically lower-
ing her head into her folded arms."[15]

Reed does not portray on the screen the final section of the novel, in which Aïssa murders Willems when he decides to be reconciled with Joanna. For myself, I think Reed made a serious mistake in ending the film at the conclusion of Part IV of the novel—with Lingard taking his final leave of Willems—rather than going on to Part V, in which Conrad depicts Willems's death at the hands of Aïssa. One might defend Reed's decision to end the film as he does by simply saying that, by this time, Willems has systematically alienated everyone he knows; and hence he is for all intents and purposes dead already. But that does not do away with the objection that, in not portraying Willems's death, Reed has failed to develop the ending of the film to its full dramatic potential, since Willems's death makes for a compelling scene in the novel, as we saw earlier. As a matter of fact, Almayer's threat to Willems earlier in the movie, that Aïssa "will kill you with her love or with her hate," seems to prefigure Aïssa's murder of Willems; but the finale of the film proves this not to be the case after all.

When I queried him about how he felt about the fact that in neither the book nor the film is Willems able to return to his wife, Reed replied that he was content to go along with Conrad on this point. "A man and a woman don't always get back together in life. I don't like to tie things up too neatly; life isn't like that."[16]

Film scholar Charles Thomas Samuels pointed out to Reed the strong critical opinion that sees *Outcast* as his best film, and went on to inquire if this film was Reed's own favorite among his pictures. Reed answered, "While I was making it, I was in love with it; but there were things that didn't come out right. It was a tricky one to do: a large production with little money."[17]

One of the few individuals associated with the film to comment on it besides Reed is Wendy Hiller, who played Mrs. Almayer. In an interview published in 1992, Ms. Hiller rightly states that her character, as created by Conrad, was a full-blooded Malay, whom the film makers turned into a white woman.[18] But Ms. Hiller is wrong in stating that the film was something of a hybrid, because it was based on two Conrad novels. This erroneous statement clearly indicates that the actress was misled by the fact that *Almayer's Folly* and *An Outcast of the Islands* are companion novels. To be specific, because of the affinities between the two works, she gratuitously assumed that the film was derived from both books.

When one considers Reed's efforts to remain faithful to the spirit of his source story in bringing *Outcast* to the screen, and one recalls, in addition, the peerless performance of Trevor Howard *(The Third Man)* as Willems, it is easy to endorse Pauline Kael's judgment of the film. She says that it is "better than any previous film drawn from Conrad's work"; what's more, Kael does not hesitate to call *Outcast* one of the most underrated of modern films, since it found little favor with the mass audience when it was first released.[19]

Furthermore, film historian William K. Everson, in his unpublished program notes on the movie, lauds the director because he did not stoop to "selling out to sex and melodrama," as a more commercially-minded director might have done. In addition, one can also praise Reed for shooting the film on location in Borneo and Ceylon, since the scenes shot on location lend an authentic flavor to the film that a Conrad film shot on the studio back lot (like the silent version of *Lord Jim*, which we shall take up later) simply does not have.

Because of the high critical reputation of the film, I have thought it wise to cite some critics' opinions about *Outcast* in this chapter, to substantiate that reputation. But perhaps Robert Moss said it all in his glowing assessment of the movie in his book on Reed. For Willems there is no redemption after he is branded as an embezzler, says Moss. Instead of redeeming himself, Willems goes on to betray the trust of Lingard, his mentor, by divulging his key trade secret to Lingard's rivals. In the wake of this ultimate treachery, writes Moss, "Willems descends even deeper into the pit; and Reed records his degradation with an uncompromising detachment that Conrad would have admired."[20]

In conclusion, one is glad to report that, although the film failed at the box office when it was originally released, it has since found a wider audience when it has been televised on PBS, where it has finally attracted some of the larger audience which it deserves.

Chapter 5

The Lower Depths: Film Versions of Conrad's Short Fiction

The Secret Sharer: The Short Story

Conrad recalls in the "Author's Note" to "The Secret Sharer" in the Collected Edition, where it appears in the volume entitled *Twixt Land and Sea Tales,* that the central episode in the story was derived from an actual happening.

When Conrad came to write the tale in 1909, he recalled an incident that had occurred in the fall of 1880 aboard the vessel *Cutty Sark,* an event about which he had read a good deal in newspaper accounts of the time. Sydney Smith, the chief mate of the ship, ordered a member of the crew, John Francis, to perform a particular duty aboard ship and Francis refused. When the mutinous Francis defied Smith further by threatening him with a club, Smith grabbed the bludgeon from Francis's hand and struck him on the head with it—a blow which ulti-mately caused the death of John Francis. Smith was confined to his quarters by the captain of the *Cutty Sark* for the rest of the voyage, and was ultimately sentenced to seven months' impris-onment for manslaughter.

In Conrad's version of the incident in "The Secret Sharer," Leggatt, the character modeled on Smith, throttles a disobedi-ent and recalcitrant crew member to death during a storm at sea. When the captain of the ship, the *Sephora,* accuses Legatt of murder and imprisons him in his quarters, Leggatt escapes from the *Sephora* by simply jumping overboard and swimming to the nearest vessel in the same waters. The vessel happens to be the one commanded by the hero of the short story.

Carl Bennett very perceptively indicates a thematic connection between "The Secret Sharer" and *Under Western Eyes,* discussed earlier in this book: "In that novel, Razumov gave the criminal Haldin up to the authorities—and as a consequence suffered for the betrayal of a fated and unwelcome partnership. In 'The Secret Sharer,' the unnamed captain/narrator is loyal to his secret double, defying all the formal structures of a lawful society to help an accused criminal."[1]

The story begins with the hero, who is never given a name, standing alone on the deck of his ship, which is anchored at the head of the Gulf of Siam. The captain, who narrates the story, says that she is floating "at the starting point of a long journey." He continues, "I had been appointed to the command only a fortnight before," while the crew "had been together eighteen months or so, and my position was of the only stranger on board. . . . But what I felt most was being a stranger to the ship; and if all the truth must be told, I was somewhat of a stranger to myself. The youngest man on board (barring the second mate), and untried as yet by a position of fullest responsibility." He concludes, "I wondered how far I should turn out faithful to the ideal conception of one's own personality every man sets up for himself secretly."[2]

The untried captain is insecure about facing his first voyage as captain of a ship; and he wonders if he has what it takes to meet the responsibilities of command, so that he will be able to fulfill that "ideal conception" of himself which every man sets up for himself. Only time will tell, for it is only in courageously confronting the challenges that he meets in the course of the journey on which he is about to embark that he will be able to prove himself qualified for command. To that extent this journey will be a voyage of self-discovery for the captain. Hence Karl writes that the story is concerned with "the arrival of the captain at a degree of maturity in which he gains self-respect and confidence."[3] The major challenge which he must meet during the voyage is deciding how to cope with having the fugitive Leggatt on board.

As Bennett opines at this point, "This unnamed captain, reflecting on an experience of years past, tells his readers of his first real command, . . . when the crisis of initiation into knowledge of his ship and his crew was complicated by an unforeseen partnership with an escaped criminal." When Leggatt secretly boards the ship and asks for asylum, the captain first off lends him a pair of his own pajamas, since Leggatt had swum to the vessel naked. Later on, when the captain prepares for bed, he dons a pair of pajamas exactly like those he has lent to the fugitive. The captain senses that a subtle communication "has been established between them," writes Bennett, and hence he subconsciously provides "his intuitively perceived 'double' with an identical sleeping-suit."[4]

Leggatt explains his situation to the captain, and the latter is sympathetic to his plight. He accordingly decides to hide Leggatt in his cabin for the time being—and Leggatt thus becomes the "secret sharer" of the captain's quarters and of his personal life while he remains on the ship.

Leggatt describes in great detail the incident aboard the *Sephora* which resulted in the death of one of the crew at his hands. The facts are these: During a prolonged storm at sea, the sailor in question had been defiant with Leggatt, who was chief mate on the *Sephora*, when he and the other crewmen were feverishly trying to save the last sail that could keep the ship running. "It was no time for gentlemanly reproof," Leggatt explains; "and so I turned round and felled him like an ox." The sailor in turn attacked Leggatt, whereupon Leggatt grabbed him "by the throat, and went on shaking him like a rat." Then a giant wave crashed over them; and after the wave had gone, Leggatt found himself still holding the man by the throat. "He was black in the face," says Leggatt. When the captain of the *Sephora* discovered what had happened, he informed Leggatt, "Mr. Leggatt, you have killed a man. You can act no longer as chief mate of this ship" (54-55).

In setting forth this episode for the captain, Leggatt makes it clear that the ship was in danger of foundering when he had his confrontation with the sailor; and under the circumstances he could not brook any disobedience from a mutinous crew member. Consequently Leggatt laid violent hands on the man in order to subdue him; but he had not intended to strangle the man, and had done so inadvertently.

While listening to Leggatt's story, the captain comments, "He appealed to me as if our experiences had been as identical as our clothes" (54). Leggatt appeals to their common experience as officers in having to cope with an insubordinate trouble-maker among the ship's crew. Furthermore, the captain feels a certain kinship with Leggatt in that he sees himself as "almost as much a stranger on board as himself" (62). The captain is a stranger to the ship since he has yet to command her on a voyage; Leggatt is a stranger to her since he is a fugitive taking temporary refuge there. Therefore, in gazing at Leggatt the captain senses that he is faced by his own reflection "in the depths of a sombre and immense mirror" (53). One can readily understand, then, why Conrad describes the story in the "Preface" to *The Shorter Tales* as one which focuses on "the *esprit de corps*, the deep fellowship of two young seamen meeting for the first time."[5]

After hearing Leggatt's account of what transpired on board the *Sephora*, the captain reflects, "I knew well enough that my double was no homicidal ruffian" (54). After all, Leggatt had not meant to kill the sailor, but to keep him from interfering with work on the ship's last sail; and in working might and main to save that sail, Leggatt had kept the vessel from shipwreck. In sum, he handled a harrowing crisis as best he could. The captain therefore decides to protect Leggatt from legal prosecution. That means, however, that Leggatt must endure life as a perpetual fugitive. For his part, Leggatt is willing to face such a life, because he feels that he is marked by the "brand of Cain"; and hence he is ready to wander the face of the earth as a vagabond and exile—which was the price that Cain paid for murdering his brother Abel (59).

Once the hero of our story has put out to sea, he eventually decides to bring his ship close enough to the nearest land, so that Leggatt can safely and unnoticed swim to shore, where he can continue his life as a fugitive. As a parting gesture, the captain gives Leggatt a floppy white hat to shield him from the sun as he wanders the earth. After Leggatt dives into the water, the captain steers his ship perilously close to land, in order to allow Leggatt to swim to safety.

When one of the crew expresses his anxiety that the captain will wreck the ship on the rocky shore, the captain sternly orders him to be silent, so that the man will not spread panic among the rest of the crew. But when the sailor insists on predicting disaster for the ship, the captain grabs the man and shakes him violently. In fact, the captain throttles this man in much the same way that Leggatt had throttled the sailor he attacked. Thus Conrad suggests that the same seeds of violence lurk within the captain that manifested themselves in Leggatt; hence we see that in yet another way Leggatt is the captain's second self. Unlike Leggatt, however, the captain releases the man before he inflicts on him any serious harm. "The protagonist cannot fully become a captain," Rising rightly remarks, "until he recognizes the existence of a Leggatt in himself."[6]

The white hat floats off Leggatt's head as he swims to shore, thereby serving fortunately as a marker to indicate the drift of the current, so that the captain will avoid bringing the vessel too close to land and thus run aground. In skillfully maneuvering the ship to safety, the captain shows himself to be in total control of the vessel. And so the insecure captain we met at the beginning of the story, who wondered if he was capable of commanding a sea-going vessel, has proved to himself that he is indeed worthy of command by weathering this crisis with skill and resourcefulness. He is therefore confident that he can handle the vessel in whatever crisis may be in store for him during the balance of the journey. For he now enjoys "the perfect communion of a seaman and his first command" (95).

Catharine Rising neatly sums up the story by saying that "a sympathetic listener hides Leggatt on his own ship and sails perilously near shore to let him escape." In short, "two young men collude to evade maritime justice and Conrad approves, for both survive."[7]

The Secret Sharer: The First Film Version

The first screen adaptation of "The Secret Sharer" was released as part of an omnibus film which also included a movie version

of Stephen Crane's "The Bride Comes to Yellow Sky," under
the overall title of *Face to Face* (1952).

The running time of John Brahm's "Secret Sharer" was kept
to under an hour. This approach to adapting the short story for
film meant that Brahm and his screenwriter could develop
Conrad's compact tale to its fullest dramatic potential on the
screen, without feeling the need to manufacture the additional
plot material which would have been required to turn the
source story into a feature-length film. Consequently, film critic
Robert Cass says of Aeneas MacKenzie's screenplay for the
Brahm "Sharer," "No extraneous characters, no additional
scenes have been written in."[8] As a result, Cass feels that this
adaptation of the story adheres very closely to the meaning and
spirit of Conrad's tale.

The movie opens with the anonymous captain, played by
James Mason *(Lolita)*, reciting, voice-over on the sound track,
some lines that appear near the beginning of the tale, while the
first page of the story is shown on the screen: "My ship lay at
anchor at the head of the Gulf of Siam. She floated at the starting point of a long journey, very still in an immense stillness,
the shadows of her spars flung far to the eastward by the setting
sun. At that moment I was alone on her decks."

Brahm cuts to a close-up of the captain at the rail of the ship
at this point, as the captain says to his ship, "You are my first
command; and you're good enough for me, old girl. The question is, am I good enough for you? Only the sea will tell." The
captain expresses his misgivings that he may not be ready for
his first command in lines which approximate those in which he
articulates these same misgivings in the story.

The movie's adherence to its literary source is especially clear
in the scene in which Leggatt (Michael Pate) describes to the
hero how he came to accidentally kill a mutinous subordinate:
"I killed a man who wouldn't do his duty and wouldn't let anyone else do theirs," says Leggatt. "I flattened him on the deck
because he had lost courage and was upsetting everyone else."
At this point Brahm inserts a flashback which depicts Leggatt
throttling the recalcitrant crew member in the midst of a hor-
rendous typhoon, as angry waves splash across the deck of the

ship. When the crewman Leggatt has strangled goes limp in death, the captain of the *Sephora* accuses Leggatt of deliberately murdering the man. Leggatt accordingly escapes from the *Sephora,* and he swims over to the hero's ship, which is anchored nearby. Brahm wisely dramatizes Leggatt's killing of the sailor—instead of having Leggatt merely recount it in words to the hero—since this flashback makes for one of the film's most exciting sequences.

The director exercises his artistic ingenuity in other ways. He employs images of imprisonment to indicate that Leggatt is considered a criminal in the eyes of the law. For example, when Leggatt recounts the story of the death of the sailor, he is photographed in medium shot through ropes on the deck which suggest prison bars. In addition, the pajamas which the captain lends to him have stripes on them that recall a prison uniform.

Brahm stages the scene in which the captain sails his ship close to shore so that Leggatt can swim safely to land, in a thrilling fashion. When the ship comes perilously near to the rocky coast, a mate named Brown expresses his terror that the ship is going to founder. When he refuses to be silenced, the captain angrily begins to throttle him—at which point Brahm inserts a shot of Leggatt shaking by the throat the mate whom he killed. This shot implies that the captain is doing just what Leggatt did under similar circumstances. When the captain comes to his senses, he releases his grip on the man immediately. The captain then guides the ship away from the shore. Brahm nicely portrays at film's end the hero's conviction that he has proved himself a worthy commanding officer by adroitly steering his ship close enough to shore to allow Leggatt to swim safely to the beach without running the vessel aground. Brahm makes this point by having one of the crew compliment the captain in the following words: "I don't hold with this hearty kind of sailing; but we now know what kind of a seaman he really is."

All in all, "The Secret Sharer" episode of *Face to Face* is a screenworthy adaptation of Conrad's short story. Now let us turn to the other film adaptation of "Secret Sharer," made two decades later.

The Secret Sharer: The Second Film Version

The second movie version of "The Secret Agent" was written and directed by Larry Yust. The film was produced for the educational market by Encyclopedia Britannica Films. Like Brahm, Yust made a mini-feature of the story. This 1973 film accordingly adheres closely to the Conrad original without the necessity of adding new plot material to the script, in order to extend the film to feature-length. Yust's film is also similar to Brahm's in that Yust opted to present the episode of Leggatt's accidental strangling of the mutinous crewman in flashback, in order to realize its full dramatic potential on the screen.

But Yust's film is quite different from Brahm's in some ways. For one thing, Yust's version of the tale follows the source story in a way that Brahm's version does not, by emphasizing the captain's conviction that Leggatt is his double. Thus the captain (David Soul) says, voice-over on the sound track, at the point when he hides Leggatt in his cabin, "I was not alone; I was there with my secret self." As a matter of fact, in one scene Yust picks up on a line in the short story in which the captain reflects, while watching Leggatt asleep in his bed, "I was constantly watching myself, . . . sleeping in that bed" (66). In the film the captain, who wears a beard, looks down at Leggatt, who is clean-shaven, as Leggatt lies sleeping in the captain's bed. Yust cuts to a close-up of Leggatt in which Leggatt sports a beard just like the captain's; this implies that the captain imagines that Leggatt has a beard like his own; then the director cuts to a short of Leggatt as he really looks: clean-shaven. This series of shots makes it clear that the captain implicitly sees Leggatt as a mirror image of himself, just as the captain does in the story.

In the climactic scene at the end of the movie Yust makes significant use of the hat which the captain gives to Leggatt when the latter leaves the ship. (By contrast, Brahm omits this important detail altogether in his film.) When Leggatt leaves the hat behind in the water as he swims to a nearby island, the captain spies it and says on the sound track, "My hat was floating there, warning me just in time that the ship was drifting back toward the island." He watches the hat float toward the shore as he stands gripping the rail. "It marks the place," he continues, "where the secret sharer of my cabin and my thoughts, my second self, swam away." Then he adds what is in fact the closing phrase of the short story, as he refers to Leggatt as a "free man, a proud swimmer, striking out for a new destiny."

It is difficult to choose which of the two film versions of "The Secret Sharer" is the better one since, after all, both are straightforward, serviceable renderings of their common source story. If one ultimately chooses the Brahm adaptation over the one directed by Yust, it is simply because the Brahm version stars James Mason, one of the most distinguished British actors of his generation; and Mason gives an immaculate performance as the hero. By contrast, David Soul gives an uninspired portrayal of the hero in the second film, simply because he is not in the same class as an actor with Mason. Hence Brahm's version of "The Secret Sharer" is the preferred one.

"Because of the Dollars": The Short Story

The other Conrad story we wish to take up deals with a fallen woman nicknamed "Laughing Anne"–an ironic nickname to be sure since Anne's sordid life is decidedly no laughing matter. As Leo Gurko observes, "She attaches herself to whatever man will live with her."

Captain Davidson, who is the skipper of a ship that sometimes docks at the port in the tropics where Anne lives, played a minor role in Conrad's novel *Victory* as Heyst's only close friend. But Davidson is the hero of the present story. As the plot unfolds, Davidson imprudently lets it be known in the waterfront bar which he visits when he is in port that he has on board his ship at present a treasure chest of coins which he is transporting back to the mainland. A Frenchman who has two stumps where his hands should be (due to an accident he was involved in some years before) overhears Davidson's ill-advised remarks and decides to rob Davidson of his rich cargo before the latter sets sail for home. Anne gets to hear of the Frenchman's plans, which include murdering Davidson if he refuses to give up the treasure; and she warns Davidson about the plot which the crippled Frenchman has hatched. When the Frenchman discovers how she has ruined his chances to steal the money, he takes his vengeance on her by smashing her skull with one of the heavy stumps that are attached to the end of his wrists. Thus Anne, Gurko concludes, "saves Captain Davidson's life at the expense of her own."[9]

This grim tale of revenge and murder was not well received by Conrad critics when it appeared in a collection of his short stories entitled *Within the Tides.* Yet Conrad thought enough of the tale to attempt to dramatize it as a two-act play under the title *Laughing Anne* in 1920, the same year in which he adapted *The Secret Agent* for the stage. But he failed to find a producer who would mount a stage production of the work.

Laughing Anne: The Play

In John Galsworthy's Introduction to the published edition of the play, he hazards that one reason why Conrad was unable to find a producer for the play was simply that "Conrad probably never realized that a man without hands would be an almost unbearable spectacle; that what you can write about freely cannot always be endured by the living eye."[10] As a matter of fact, I can attest that, having seen *Laughing Anne* on the screen, if not on the stage, the spectacle of a man who has two grotesque stumps where his hands ought to be was a pretty gruesome sight. John Batchelor notes that an additional reason that the play went unproduced was that it required elaborate sets, and even a ship onstage.[11]

Be that as it may, Conrad's stage version of the tale was quite faithful to the spirit of his original story—as one might expect when the playwright in question also happens to be the same writer who wrote the story in the first place.

The only significant element of the short story's plot that Conrad omitted from the play concerns Anne's young son Tony, who is left an orphan in the wake of her death. In the original story Davidson feels morally obligated to care for the child, since the boy's mother saved his life. But Davidson's wife, who is obsessively jealous of him, concludes quite gratuitously that Tony is her husband's illegitimate offspring and accordingly refuses to take the lad into her home. As a matter of fact,

Davidson's wife has always despised living in the tropics; and so she ultimately uses her outrage over the child as a convenient excuse to leave her husband and go home to her parents. The story concludes with Tony having grown into a fine young man with aspirations to be a missionary.

The only reference to this episode in the play is in Davidson's curtain line, in which he muses that Anne is on his conscience and hence he will see to it that her boy has his chance in life. It is not surprizing that Conrad declined to dramatize this last section of the original story, since it is little more than an epilogue to the story proper, which really is over, for all practical purposes, with the death of Anne.

Now let us turn to the movie which was later made from the tale, which was likewise fairly faithful to Conrad's story.

Laughing Anne: The Film

The movie version of the story, which was directed in 1954 by Herbert Wilcox *(Trent's Last Case)*, starred Margaret Lockwood *(The Lady Vanishes)* in the title role. Wendell Corey and Forrest Tucker lent her support as Captain Davidson and Jim Ferrell, the man without the hands, respectively. The one truly distinguishing characteristic of the film is that it represents the only time when Conrad himself was portrayed in a film adaptation of one of his fictional works. Robert Harris enacts the role of the novelist who narrates the story of Anne to some friends in a series of flashbacks while they are sharing a drink in a café.

Conrad, as portrayed in the film, is not an internal (subjective) narrator; i.e., he is not telling his own personal experiences and giving his own subjective reactions to them (as does the narrator of the film *Apocalypse Now*). He is rather an external (objective) narrator, narrating the life of someone else, in this case, that of Laughing Anne. As Avrom Fleishman describes an external (objective) narrator, such a narrator tends "to deliver a historical statement or objective version—the story as it really happened."[12]

Conrad is introduced as the narrator at the beginning of the film with the following brief preparatory statement: "Some years ago in any seaboard town, city, or settlement east of Suez you might have met Joseph Conrad, a Pole by birth, a seaman by choice, and a writer by chance. Because he knew the ways of the human heart were as many and as devious as those of the sea which he loved, Conrad became one of the greatest story-tellers of his generation. This is one of his stories. . . ."

The task confronting a screenwriter charged with creating a script for a feature-length film from a short story is a formidable one, as A. E. Hotchner suggests in the Introduction to this book. After all, the scripter must invent a sufficient amount of additional material to stretch the original story into a full-length feature—without at the same time totally obliterating the point of the original story amid the intricacies of the extended story-line.

The tendency of a screenwriter working on a short story is to put in additional incidents merely to lengthen the script, instead of developing the characters or the plot in greater depth, in order to enable the viewer to gain a deeper under-standing of the characters and the motivation of their behavior. This is precisely what happened in the case of *Laughing Anne*. Nevertheless, one does not envy screenwriter Pamela Bowers when she was faced with the task of lengthening this poignant short story into a feature-length film. Indeed, I must admit a certain admiration for the scenarist's ingenuity in inventing a number of additional episodes to fill out the plot of Conrad's story for screen presentation as a full-length film. Still, it seems to me that she has fulfilled her task, not wisely but too well; for the resulting film is top-heavy with extra plot material.

For example, in "Because of the Dollars" Conrad offers a brief—but sufficient—explanation of how the Frenchman came to lose his hands: "His hands had been blown away by a dyna-mite cartridge while he was fishing in some lagoon. This acci-dent . . . had made him more wicked than before, which is say-ing a good deal."[13] By contrast, the film spends a great amount of screen time depicting how Jem Ferrell (the name of the man without hands in the film—he is nameless in the story) came to lose his hands.

We learn in a lengthy flashback that Jem was once a boxer and that he fell in love with Laughing Anne, who at that point in her life was a singer in a bar that Jem frequented. Before an important bout a gambler bribed Jem to throw the fight. But Anne, for her part, did not want Jem to turn crooked, and so she discouraged Jem from throwing the fight. Jem accordingly won the match that he had agreed to lose in order to live up to Anne's expectations of him as a sportsman.

Because Jem ultimately declined to lose the fight he had committed himself to lose, the irate gambler sends a passel of his henchmen to the café, where Jem is having a drink after the bout, to rough him up. As Jem slugs it out with the gambler's minions, a flying whiskey bottle, presumably aimed at Jem by one of the thugs, smashes against a huge mirror which is hanging on the wall, and it falls on Jem and crushes his hands beyond recognition. Anne later comments when she recalls this incident, "His hands were crushed, cut to pieces. Poor Jem—the championship of the world was within his grasp, cut he had no hands to grasp it with."

The film bogs down in the endless flashback that dramatizes how Jem came to lose his hands, whereas Conrad's brief explanation of the incident in the short story is quite enough to describe what happened. It is therefore fair to say that *Laughing Anne* would have been a better movie had the film makers placed the ending of the film somewhat closer to its beginning by shortening the long flashback that portrays Anne and Jem's past life together.

As this elaborate and over-long expository flashback draws to a close, the film returns to the main action in the present, in which Anne tips Davidson off to Jem's plan to murder him and steal the treasure that has been entrusted to him. Jem accordingly gets even with her by smashing her head with one of his heavy stumps.

Jerry Vermilye describes the film as "an inferior adaptation of Joseph Conrad's *Between the Tides*." In point of fact, the film is an adaptation of one story in the collection of stories entitled *Between the Tides*. Be that as it may, Vermilye goes on to explain that Anne is "an 1890s chanteuse drifting with her ex-boxer lover through the exotic world of South Seas waterfront saloons. Schooner captain [Davidson] then makes it a love triangle." The film ends, Vermilye concludes, with "a melodramatic twist that kills off Lockwood."[14]

Vermilye suggests that the reason that Anne warns Davidson of Jem's plot to kill him and steal the treasure is that she has fallen in love with him. Although there is no indication in the short story that Davidson ever feels anything but compassion for Anne, in the movie it is made clear that a love relationship has gradually grown up between them. Hence in the film Anne gives her life for the man she really loves.

It is significant to note that the film, like Conrad's play, omits the episode that focuses on the plight of Anne's son Tony after his mother's death, and the refusal of Davidson's wife to provide for him. For this episode would have needlessly extended the length of the film. In fact, Davidson's wife becomes estranged from him early in the film and accordingly goes back to England. That leaves Davidson free to fall in love with Anne.

In the movie, as in the short story, Davidson feels obligated to take care of Tony. Hence Conrad comments, voice-over on the sound track, that Davidson was "more than a father to Laughing Anne's boy. He taught him the ways of the sea; and ever since the young man has known his own mind, he has wanted only one thing: to be a sailor" like Davidson. These remarks introduce the film's concluding shot: David and Tony, now a teenager, standing on the deck of a ship. Davidson begins to tell him a story about his mother, and the boy laughs uproariously with the laugh of Laughing Anne.

This brief epilogue attempts to provide the semblance of a happy conclusion for the film, in the wake of Anne's tragic death. The happy ending consists in the fact that Laughing Anne lives on in her son and that Davidson loves the lad as he had loved his mother.

One cannot question the serious intent of the film. Indeed one of the definite merits of the movie is that it recalls Conrad's ongoing theme of redemption through sacrifice, as already mentioned at the outset of this book. In this instance, the present film depicts how Anne redeems her immoral past by paying with her life to save Davidson from being murdered in cold blood by Jem.

My criticism of the movie as somewhat overlength, however, is backed up by the reviewer of the movie in *Variety* (May 5, 1954), who emphasizes how the pace of the film seems too slow, even though the movie's actual running time is only ninety minutes. Perhaps the reviewer in *The New York Times* (May 8, 1954) says it all when he dismisses the film's "lusterless" script as a "plodding account of thwarted love, sacrifice, and skullduggery." Moreover, in manufacturing a love affair between Davidson and Anne, the film departs noticeably from the original story, in a way that Conrad's stage dramatization does not.

In sum, *Laughing Anne* ranks among the lesser films which have been made from Conrad's fiction to date. By contrast, we now turn to examine not one but two adaptations of Conrad's novel *Lord Jim,* both of which are deserving of close critical examination.

Chapter 6

The Disenchanted:
Lord Jim (1925 and 1965)

Lord Jim: The Novel

Conrad concludes the "Author's Note" to *Lord Jim* in the Collected Edition by recalling that "one sunny morning" in 1888 he encountered one Augustus Podmore Williams, the seaman on whom he modeled Lord Jim, "in the commonplace surroundings of an Eastern roadstead. I saw his form pass by, perfectly silent."[1] Conrad then goes on to say that he was fascinated by this glimpse of Williams, who at this juncture in his life was an agent of a merchant selling supplies to incoming ships, because of the rumors he had heard about Williams around the waterfront where his ship was docked.

Eight years earlier, in July 1880, Williams was first officer on a ship called the *Jeddah*, which was transporting close to a thousand pilgrims to Mecca. On August 2, the decrepit vessel ran into a gale, during which both the boilers shook loose and the engines had to be shut down. On August 8, the captain reluctantly decided that the ship was going to founder, and ordered his officers and crew to man the lifeboats. As it happened, there were not enough lifeboats aboard the *Jeddah* to accommodate all the passengers, so the pilgrims were left behind to fend for themselves while the officers rowed their own lifeboat for shore.

The lifeboat occupied by the officers of the *Jeddah* was eventually picked up by another British steamer and taken to Aden, where the captain reported that the ship had sunk, and that all of the passengers had gone down with the ship. Much to the chagrin of the officers of the *Jeddah*, the ship was towed into the harbor on the following day by yet another British vessel—with all of the pilgrims safely on board.

The cowardly behavior of Williams and the others was condemned in newspaper editorials around the world, and the scandal was still being talked about when Conrad set eyes upon Williams eight years after the calamity. (As a matter of fact, Conrad had seen the *Jeddah*, which was still afloat, in the harbor at Singapore on March 22, 1883.)

Like *The Secret Agent, Lord Jim* began its literary life as a short story entitled. "Jim: A Sketch." But Conrad altered the title of the story to *Lord Jim: A Tale* when the story began to reach the proportions of a novel. In the book Jim's life is depicted in a series of flashbacks which are not presented in chronological order. In the course of the novel Charles Marlow, a seaman who narrates the bulk of the novel, endeavors to bring together all of the known facts he can muster about Jim. The events of Jim's life are thus revealed by a number of witnesses, none of whom knows the whole story about Jim; and their recollections are presented in flashback. Accordingly Marlow—and the reader—must piece together the facts about Jim as they come to light. In the end Marlow feels that he has presented a coherent picture of Jim. "My information was fragmentary," he says near the conclusion of the novel; "but I've fitted the pieces together, and there are enough of them to make an intelligible picture" (343).

One point that Marlow emphasizes about Jim is that he had a very active imagination which he employed to manufacture daydreams in which he performed heroic deeds. When Jim fantasized, Marlow notes, "his thoughts would be full of valorous deeds: he loved these dreams and the success of his imaginary achievements." These daydreams fostered in him an unbounded confidence in himself. In his arrogance, Jim was convinced that "there was nothing he could not face." Ross Murfin writes that, as things turn out, "Jim just happens to be unable . . . to be in life what he is" in his daydreams.[2] In fact, Jim's idealized image of himself is shattered when he commits an act of cowardice aboard a ship named the *Patna* as a young officer; and he is dogged his whole life by the disgraceful behavior he exhibited on that occasion.

This act of cowardice is the same one that Williams had perpetrated in real life: The officers—Jim included—fear that the *Patna,* which is loaded with pilgrims, is going to sink when the vessel's bulkhead springs a leak in a storm; and they desert the ship. In an attempt to explain—not to condone—Jim's action, Marlow explains that Jim panicked during this crisis because his overactive imagination played him false by exaggerating the perilousness of the situation: "His confounded imagination had evoked for him all the horrors of panic, the trampling rush, the pitiful screams, [life]boats swamped—all the appalling incidents of a disaster at sea he had ever heard of" (88).

As a result, Jim joins the vile captain and his seedy officers in escaping from the *Patna* in a lifeboat. Murfin writes, "He falls a distance far greater than the one from the deck of the *Patna* to the ocean's surface."[3] Marlow phrases it this way: "He had tumbled from a height he could never scale again" (112). Jim and the others eventually reach shore. As in the case of the real-life incident from which *Lord Jim* is derived, the officers and crew of the *Patna* are ashamed to see the vessel which they had abandoned being brought safely to port on the day after they arrived on shore. Jim feels it is his duty in conscience to endure the public disgrace of appearing before the official court of inquiry held after the notorious *Patna* affair by the maritime authorities.

Marlow sees Jim for the first time during the period when the court of inquiry, which is investigating the *Patna* debacle, is in session. His first reaction to Jim is that he is "one of us." Gurko explains this phrase in his book on Conrad by saying that Marlow is referring to "the community of white Europeans struggling to maintain their favored position among the Asiatic Malays. . . . Jim is white, English, youthful, handsome, rugged looking; he looks like 'one of us.'"[4] But, as Marlow is at pains to point out, Jim's appearance is deceiving. "There he stood," Marlow says of his first view of Jim, "clean-limbed, clean-faced, firm on his feet, as promising a boy as the sun ever shone on. . . . He had no business to look so sound. I thought to myself—well, if this sort could go wrong like that" (40). Marlow concludes, "He looked as genuine as a new sovereign, but there was some infernal alloy in his metal" (45). On the surface, Jim appears to be an upright seaman, whose behavior is beyond reproach. Yet, as he demonstrated during the *Patna* episode, he is quite capable of disgraceful behavior. Consequently, Jim is like a coin that looks genuine, but has some counterfeit metal in its composition.

By the same token, Marlow observes on another occasion that Jim looks "spotlessly neat, apparelled in immaculate white from shoes to hat" (3). Since white symbolizes purity, Jim's spotless appearance implies that he is a man of impeccable character. But his white apparel belies how his conduct has stained his character.

At all events, Jim admits his guilt during the proceedings of the court of inquiry and accepts the consequences: His certificate as a seaman is forthwith revoked. Capt. Brierly, the chief judge at the court of inquiry, is very disturbed by the fact that he is compelled to condemn a fellow naval officer for dereliction of duty, since, as Gurko comments, the public spectacle of the trial dramatizes "before the natives the downfall of a white man"—one of us.[5]

Brierly subsequently becomes obsessed with the notion that, if he had had to confront a crisis similar to the one that Jim had to face, he might not have acquitted himself any better than Jim did. Fearing that the same seeds of cowardice which lurked inside of Jim are also inside of him, he is terrified that he too might desert his post during a catastrophe at sea. Therefore he is later driven, during a subsequent sea voyage, to drown himself in mid-ocean, so that such a personal disaster could never overtake him. Murfin remarks that Brierly makes Marlow wonder if the *Patna* episode has destroyed Brierly's confidence in himself and, beyond that, in the possibility of human beings so decent that no situation could make them cower or act like scoundrels." In short, "Brierly . . . sees himself in Jim."[6]

For his part, Jim tries to live down his personal disgrace by fleeing to the unmapped jungles of Borneo in the Malay Archipelago, to an island called Patusan, where his shameful transgression is unknown; and he accordingly sets about making a new life for himself on the island. In due course the natives who live on Patusan look to Jim as a sage and courageous leader—whom they christen *Tuan Jim* (Lord Jim)—as he more and more takes responsibility for governing their tribe with their unqualified support.

Misfortune strikes again, however, when an infamous pirate known as Gentleman Brown and his notorious band of cutthroats sail into the port ostensibly to get supplies in order to continue their voyage, but really with a view to pillaging the town before going on their way. Fearing that Brown and his marauding band of pirates will violently sack the town and its inhabitants before continuing their voyage, Jim's own native counsellors vote to drive away Brown and his gang in a gun battle before they have a chance to loot the townspeople.

Jim has a private confrontation with Brown in which Brown shrewdly suggests that there is a common bond between them since he suspects that Jim too has been guilty of some crime in the past. A white man like Jim, says Brown, would not have isolated himself on a remote island if he was not hiding from his past. "I won't ask you what scared you into this infernal hole," Brown declares; but he is convinced that Jim is guilty of some behavior he is ashamed of (383).

Brown secretly feels that his little band of brigands has little chance of winning a pitched battle with the native warriors, and hence he promises Jim to depart from the island peacefully, without engaging in battle with the tribesmen. Brown tells Jim that, as a man with a shady past, Jim has no right to be so high and mighty that he will not trust Brown's promise to do as he says, just because he too has a dark past.

As Marlow summarizes Brown's remarks to Jim, "He asked Jim whether he had nothing fishy in his life to remember that he was so damnably hard upon a man trying to get out of a deadly hole by the first means that came to hand. . . . And there ran through the rough talk a vein of subtle reference to their common blood, an assumption of common experience, a sickening suggestion of common guilt, of secret knowledge that was like a bond of their minds and hearts" (387). As Murfin comments, "Seeing Jim as a hypocrite who had probably come to Patusan because of some crime as bad as those he himself had committed, Brown appealed to Jim's fear that the two of them were brothers in imperfection."[7]

Jim accordingly decides to trust Brown, and allow him and his men to leave the island without a battle in the hope that bloodshed can be avoided. He wishes to act responsibly in protecting the lives of the natives of Patusan in an effort to atone in some way for having shirked his responsibility to protect the lives of the passengers of the *Patna*. Jim communicates his decision to Doramin, the chieftain of the native tribe; and he even pledges to Doramin and the other elders of the tribe that if any of the citizens of Patusan are killed by Brown and his men, he will forfeit his own life to pay for any life that is lost.

Brown and his crew apparently leave the port peacefully, while Dain Waris—Doramin's son and Jim's best friend—and his warriors watch from shore. But Brown orders his men to open fire on Dain Waris and the other tribesmen along the shore; and Dain Waris, among others, dies on the spot. Presumably the irredeemably evil Brown did not keep his word to leave Patusan without any bloodshed because he was angry that he and his men did not get a chance to plunder the town as they had planned to do, and this was his way of venting his rage. In any case, Jim now must live up to his pledge to forfeit his life in exchange for the lives that have been lost.

As Gurko writes, Jim "gives Brown and his ruffians leave to depart in peace. This turns out to be a mistake in judgment, a fatal mistake that leads to the murder of [Dain Waris] and others." But, adds Gurko, Jim "pays for his mistake without wavering."[8] And Marlow comments, "Everything was gone, and he had been once more unfaithful to his trust, had lost again all men's confidence" (409). Jim is aware that the only way to regain the confidence of the tribesmen that he has lost is to make good his promise to give up his life in exchange for the lives of those who have perished because of his poor judgment. And so he resolutely presents himself to Doramin and stands unflinchingly before him as the chieftain shoots him to death.

When Jim settled in Patusan, he had yet to live down the incident on the *Patna*. As a matter of fact, that incident was implicitly recalled by the very fact that the word *Patna* is contained in the word *Patusan*. And thus Patusan, as an anagram of *Patna*, recalled for Jim the shame which that episode had visited upon him. But in courageously accepting death at novel's end,

Marlow suggests, Jim has at last redeemed himself by wiping away his past cowardice and shown himself to be the brave man he at last has become. Murfin concludes, "If we believe that . . . Marlow has rescued some truth from the obscurity of Jim's story—then we may well believe that Jim, too, has succeeded in the moment that he seemed to have failed"; i.e., the moment of his death.[9]

Lord Jim (1925): The Silent Film

The silent film of *Lord Jim* (1925) serves notice at the outset that it intends to be a faithful rendition of Conrad's novel with the following printed prologue: "This is a sincere attempt to put on the screen the best-known and best-loved work of the master novelist Joseph Conrad."

It is gratifying to report that this film, directed by Victor Fleming *(Gone with the Wind)* almost lives up to that pledge. As a matter of fact, screenwriter John Russell is to be commended for combining the character of the captain of the *Patna* with the character of Gentleman Brown into a single character called Capt. Brown (played by Noah Beery, Sr.). Accordingly Capt. Brown the pirate stands as a living reminder of the erstwhile captain of the *Patna* and his connection with Jim's cowardly behavior aboard the *Patna*.

In addition, Fleming is careful to emphasize in the film a visual symbol that is taken right from the novel. He does so in this manner: Early in the novel a trader named Stein, a mutual friend of Jim and Doramin, gives Jim (Percy Marmount) a ring that Doramin had once given Stein as a keepsake. At the climax of the film, when Jim sends word through a native servant to Dain Waris that he has decided to allow Brown and his men to leave Patusan unmolested, he instructs the servant to give Dain Waris the same ring, which indicates that the message the servant is delivering does in fact come from Jim. Dain Waris in turn puts the ring on his own finger when he receives it, as a token of the fact that he accepts the message as coming directly from Jim himself, and that he trusts Jim's judgment in the matter.

In the epilogue of the movie, after Dain Waris and others have been slaughtered by Brown and his gang, Jim faces Doramin in the presence of Dain Waris's corpse, which is lying on a stretcher before them. He takes the ring from Dain Waris's finger and drops it into Doramin's lap, as a sign that he will keep his promise to redeem his pledge of forfeiting his life for the life of Dain Waris and the other native warriors who have died. The ring then rolls off of Doramin's lap and onto the floor near Dain Waris's corpse. As Jim looks disconsolately at the ring lying in the dust, he realizes at this point in the story that it no longer serves as an emblem of trust between white man and native; for Jim has forfeited the trust of Doramin and his tribe. Hence the ring deserves to be trodden underfoot. Jeanine Basinger notes that Fleming possessed "a skillful sense of storytelling through the camera." Fleming's strong sense of visual storytelling is certainly on display in the present film, particularly in the deft symbolism associated with the ring, just described.[10]

Most film critics agreed when the film was released that the silent version of *Lord Jim* was a faithful adaptation of the novel. The *New York Times* review by Mordaunt Hall was the most eloquent in endorsing the film as vintage Conrad. Hall declares that the film is a "pictorial achievement throughout, which the genius of the original shines through." His rave notice goes on to say that "the handling of the script by Victor Fleming, the director, deserves unstinted praise." Hall continues by saying that "the scenic effects are so good that one might think that this production, filmed in Hollywood, was really produced in that unpleasant corner of the earth so trenchantly described by Conrad: There are the bamboo huts, the shaky bridges, the canoes, the gaudy costumes, etc."[11]

At the risk of seeming to carp, I am bound to say that the sequences that were set on the island of Patusan had all the earmarks of being shot on the studio back lot, which has more than its share of moth-eaten vegetation. Some location shooting could have been done on nearby Catalina Island—where much of the later Conrad film *Dangerous Paradise* was to be shot—and doing so would have helped immeasurably to create a realistic atmosphere for the film. As Graham Greene once wrote, somewhat sardonically, in reviewing a film that was supposedly set in mid-ocean, but was really filmed in the studio tank: "We still read in little books on the cinema, 'The film, as compared with the play, has the advantage of real backgrounds.'"[12] As Greene suggests, film makers do not always take advantage of the opportunity—denied to stage directors—to use authentic outdoor locations; certainly the silent film of *Lord Jim* did not.

At all events Hall concludes quite rightly that it is gratifying that Fleming's *Lord Jim* "has been filmed with due respect to Conrad's genius."[13]

Lord Jim (1965): The Sound Version

The sound version of *Lord Jim* (1965), made forty years after the silent version, enjoyed a number of production values that the original movie did not have. Thus the 1965 *Lord Jim* had the advantage, not only of sound, but also of widescreen, color, and shooting on authentic locations from Hong Kong to Cambodia. Indeed, one critic noted that "location shots add greatly to the effective atmosphere, and the film is made on a grand scale, and its color and widescreen are well adapted for such material."[14]

The second film was written and directed by Richard Brooks *(In Cold Blood)*. As a matter of fact, Brooks had wanted to film *Lord Jim* for several years, having admired the novel since he read it in college. Indeed, he repeatedly took options on the screen rights of the novel for eight years before he finally got the chance to mount a production of *Jim,* and then spent another three-and-a-half years writing the script and directing the film. In *Lord Jim,* says Frank Frost in his unpublished doctoral thesis on Brooks—which is still the only book-length study of the director—Brooks "saw an opportunity to pay tribute to a great writer, and to tell a story of universal appeal, regarding mankind's consistent struggle for honor, redemption, and integrity," a theme, as we know, that was close to Conrad's heart.[15]

Indeed, while he was adapting *Lord Jim* to the screen, Brooks was conscious of his responsibility to Conrad in making as accurate a film version of *Jim* as he could. As he put it, the director must respect the source story he is telling on the screen for the simple reason that "you have nothing to direct until you have a story." And he went on to say, "I think that directing is an extension of writing with film. . . . You begin to take a story and put it on film. What you are doing is writing with film."

Nevertheless, Brooks was acutely aware that filmgoers familiar with the book would complain about the changes he would make in the novel in the course of translating it to the film medium. "Why did you change it?" he could hear them saying. "It's a great book which everybody loves." Brooks says that he would respond to this objection in this fashion: "Well, you don't mean to change it; but you have to, because a film is something different from a book."[16]

One definite change which Brooks made in the novel while composing his screenplay was to tell the story in chronological order.

In the novel Jim's life is revealed to Marlow, the narrator, by a series of witnesses, each of whom has known Jim at a different stage of his life; and their memories of him are depicted in a series of flashbacks which are not presented in chronological order. As noted above, both Marlow and the reader must accordingly fit together the events of Jim's life as they come to light. In sum, the reader must piece together the jigsaw puzzle of Jim's life as he fits the various incidents that he learns about him into their proper places in the narrative.

Brooks felt that the mass audience would find the plot of the film hard to follow if the episodes of Jim's life were presented out of chronological sequence, as they are in the novel. He therefore opted to depict the events of Jim's life in the order in which they occurred, in order to allow the filmgoer to follow Jim's adventures more easily. (The silent version of the story is also told in chronological order.) As Brooks notes, he believes in rearranging the events of a novel like *Lord Jim,* "so that they tell a straighter storyline."[17]

Brooks brought over Marlow from the book to narrate the film, voice-over on the sound track, so that Marlow could comment on Jim's behavior, as he does in the novel. Thus Marlow (Jack Hawkins) is heard saying at the beginning of the film's opening credits, "Joseph Conrad wrote that if you want to know the age of the world, look at the sea in a storm. It could also show you the heart of a man. Of all those heroes and villains washed up on the shore, none was more praised or damned than Lord Jim."

Brooks wrote in the program notes which were produced for the premiere engagements of the film that movies are "an arrangement of images. In a film, words are secondary to the *visual* expression of feelings and ideas. . . . Hence the necessity of translating the profound, intricate prose style of Joseph Conrad's *Lord Jim* to the more elemental medium of images."[18] In rethinking the novel for the screen, Brooks came up with some fine visual images to underline the meaning of a scene or to point up what Jim (Peter O'Toole) is thinking.

For example, Marlow says on the sound track that Jim "had flights of fancy," at which point we see a split screen with Jim on the left-hand side daydreaming. On the right-hand side we see what he is fantasizing about: He is pictured fighting a duel with some rogue in order to save Marlow's life. The split-screen image indicates visually that Jim has an overactive imagination by which he produces heroic fantasies about himself that encourage him to foster an idealized self-image.

The first time Jim sees the *Patna*, his jaw drops in astonishment when he observes the rusty old crate of a ship that is facing him. This visual image suggests Jim's concern about the ship's capacity for survival in rough weather, a concern that returns to haunt Jim during the storm at sea, when he fears that the *Patna* is going to founder.

During the storm sequence in the film, Brooks follows Conrad's lead in showing how Jim's imagination works against him by goading him to panic. Brooks accomplishes this by utilizing some vivid visual imagery. A nervous sailor named Robinson shows Jim a leak in the bulkhead; and Jim is appalled, since he perceives that his worst fears about the *Patna* are being realized. At this point Marlow comments over the sound track that Jim had become "infected with another man's terror." Marlow adds shortly afterward, "Jim was confronted with the unexpected: his imagination made him see what he feared to see." At this moment we see Jim looking at water seeping through the leak in the bulkhead, which is the reality of the situation. Then we cut to a shot of water deluging from the bulkhead, which is what Jim *imagines* is happening; finally we cut back to the water seeping in, as before. This series of shots clearly implies how Jim's overheated imagination is getting the better of him and makes him think that the old ship is going to burst at the seams at any moment.

The captain and the other officers jump from the ship into the lifeboat that is floating beside the ship, and they shout at Jim to join them. Jim momentarily hesitates to follow their advice when he realizes that the ship's wheel, which is used to steer the vessel, has been left unattended. For a second he thinks that possibly he should stay on board and man the wheel in a desperate effort to steer the ship through the storm. But Jim ultimately decides that endeavoring to guide the ship to safety is a hopeless task, and so he too jumps into the lifeboat. The image of the abandoned ship's wheel comes back to haunt Jim later in the film since it is the emblem of his cowardice.

Marlow refers to Jim early in the movie as "one of us," a term that he uses about Jim in the book. It means, in brief, that Jim is an able British seaman who can always be counted on to do the right thing. Ironically, as Hollis Alpert wrote in his review of the film, "When the time came to display his traditional breeding, Jim did the wrong thing": He failed to do his duty on the *Patna*.[19]

After Jim's certificate as a seaman has been cancelled by the court of inquiry, Capt. Brierly, the chief judge of the court, makes an acrid remark to Jim that recalls Marlow's earlier comment: "You are one of us." But Brierly adds, "Your disgrace reflects on all of us." Sometime later, Jim picks up a newspaper on a wharf and sees Brierly's suicide headlined. Capt. Brierly, the newspaper states, left a note in his ship's log before he jumped to his death in the sea; it read, "Fear can find the flaw in any of us." In this way, Brierly explains that he wanted to drown himself, rather than live to disgrace himself as Jim had done. Brooks's inclusion of the Briefly episode in the film demonstrates his interest in portraying even minor incidents from the book, so long as they are meaningful and thought-provoking.

Brooks invented two compelling sequences for the film which underscore Jim's determination to regain the honor he lost aboard the *Patna,* by meeting any challenge that confronts him with all the courage he can muster. Therefore the two added sequences are totally in keeping with the overall thrust of Conrad's novel.

In the first sequence Jim happens to be on a boat freighted with explosives that is docked in some Malayan harbor. Suddenly the boat catches fire, which means that its cargo of gunpowder could explode at any moment and wreak havoc in the harbor. Jim keeps his head and begins beating out the flames with his jacket. Then he grabs a hatchet and smashes some beer casks which are also on board, allowing the beer to pour out of the kegs and put out the blaze. The other boats at portside toot their whistles and the bystanders on the dock cheer in order to celebrate Jim's bravery, while he cheerfully drinks a basin of beer.

A trader named Stein (Paul Lukas) asks Jim if he would like the job of transporting the gunpowder to the island of Patusan, where the natives need it to protect themselves from a gang of bandits, who are terrifying the countryside. The native tribesmen need ammunition, Stein explains, so that their skirmishes with the bandits will not be a matter of "spears against guns." Jim agrees to take the explosives to Patusan, where he hopes to get a fresh start in life, in the wake of the *Patna* debacle. As Marlow observes on the sound track, "Rich or poor, strong or weak, who among us has not begged God for a second chance?"

This brings us to the second sequence which Brooks created for the film in order to demonstrate Jim's resolve to live down his past cowardice. In this sequence Jim has to cope with the bandit chief, who is known as the General (Eli Wallach). The General, who temporarily holds Jim captive in his fort, is determined to steal the explosives which Jim has supplied for the people of Patusan to ward off the General and his bandit horde. Jim has buried the ammunition in the natives' compound, and steadfastly refuses to reveal where it is, even under torture.

In his effort to intimidate Jim into breaking down under torture, the General delivers the most chilling speech in the film:

"No man is a stranger to fear. Fear is the perfect tool for persuasion. Now, what do you fear most? What do you prize most? Your strong, young body? Your manhood? Your sight? I could make you cheat a friend, forsake honor, desert a post of duty. What fear could turn you into a coward?" As Frank Frost comments, "Jim has already deserted a post of duty, and his greatest fear is that he will do it again."[20]

As Jim is tortured at the stake, Brooks intercuts with the torture scene a judo match which is going on nearby. One of the native opponents is being mercilessly pummeled by the other, but he staunchly refuses to lie down. This fighter thus becomes a symbol of Jim's determination not to give in to the General, and in fact he does not. Jim shortly afterwards escapes from the fort, with the help of one of the natives.

If the torture scene just described was adroitly invented by Brooks, Jim's confrontation with Gentleman Brown (James Mason), the Bible-reading cut-throat, comes right out of the book. Brown attempts to convince Jim to allow him and his cohorts to depart from Patusan without bloodshed by assuring Jim that in this fashion many lives will be spared. This argument strikes a chord in Jim, who feels responsible for the lives of the people of Patusan, as he once felt responsible for saving the lives of the passengers aboard the *Patna*. This is precisely what Jim means when he says, on reflection, that on this night "the *Patna*, that phantom ship, has come to settle an old account."

As in the novel, so in the film, Brown suggests that he and Jim are linked by a common sense of guilt; i.e., both of them have done things in the past which they are ashamed of. V. F. Perkins describes Jim and Brown at this point, as they stand together on a raft, as follows:

"While they talk, Jim, fair-haired and dressed in light colors, faces out across the water, raising his right hand to lean against the raft's guide-rail. Then Brown, a swarthy, black-bearded figure in a bowler hat and dark suit, takes up the same position—except that he holds to the rail with his left hand. The image is briefly shown, but it lasts long enough for us to appreciate the psychological implications of its structure: Brown is Jim's dark reflection, his unrecognized mirror-image."

In other words, Brown reflects Jim's darker self—the side of Jim's personality that led to his shameful behavior aboard the Patna.

Perkins further comments that "the director can scarcely be given credit for the thought that shapes this image. It is an aspect of the Jim-Brown relationship that Conrad suggests in the novel from which the film derives, and one which Conrad commentators have explored at some length. Brooks invented not the idea but the image which expresses it in movie terms."[21]

Brown further suggests, quite hypocritically, that he wants a chance to prove that he can make a pledge and live up to it. "Have you never needed a second chance?" he asks Jim, thereby recalling for the viewer Marlow's comment early in the film that Jim had desperately wanted "a second chance" after the *Patna* disaster. Hence this remark of Brown's likewise hits home when Jim hears it; and he accepts Brown's promise to him that he and his men will depart from Patusan peacefully—a promise that the wily Brown, of course, does not keep. Brown, it develops, only agreed to leave the island peacefully, so that he could return secretly and launch a sneak attack on the inhabitants, with a view to carrying off some loot with him.

Brooks, who has been fairly faithful to Conrad throughout the film, remains true to his literary source by retaining the novel's tragic ending. For Jim must pay with his own life at film's end for trusting the word of a river pirate, who finally causes the death of Dain Waris, the tribal leader's son. Still Brooks would have been more faithful to the novel in the film's final passages, had he used the visual symbol of the ring of Doramin the tribal chieftain. The symbolic value of the ring which passes from Doramin to Jim and to Dain Waris in the novel could have been mined in the present movie as it was in the silent version of *Jim.* But Brooks unaccountably ignored in his adaptation of the novel the rich meaning that the ring has in the book.

In any event, his friends encourage Jim to leave Patusan before Doramin compels him to forfeit his life to pay for the death of his son Dain Waris, killed by one of Brown's henchmen. But Jim is convinced that he can no longer run away from death as he did when he deserted the *Patna;* and hence he stays on to face death. Death, then, becomes the final affirmation of Jim's honor. As Alpert has written of the second *Jim,* if Jim must accept death to regain his honor, "then he will accept it." Given his chance to go to death heroically, "Jim remembers the *Patna* and makes his choice."[22]

In preserving in his film the sad ending of the book, Brooks is thereby remaining faithful to the theme of Conrad's fiction that one achieves redemption by sacrifice and suffering. In both book and film Jim redeems himself for his dishonorable behavior aboard the *Patna* by sacrificing his life for his code of honor.

The second film version of *Jim* is in some ways a better movie than the first, not only because it boasts production values that the first film did not enjoy, but because of the top-flight cast Brooks has assembled for the film. John Baxter, in his recent essay on Brooks says, "Brooks's literary adaptations are sustained by bravura performances."[23] Baxter's observation certainly holds up when one examines the cast of *Lord Jim,* beginning with Peter O'Toole's performance in the title role. Admittedly Percy Marmount is an adequate Jim in the first film, but he is no match for Peter O'Toole *(Lawrence of Arabia)* in the second film. Indeed, O'Toole does not so much play the part of Jim as inhabit it, so attuned is he to every nuance of the role. In considering the cast of the 1965 *Lord Jim,* one must not overlook James Mason's impeccable performance as Gentleman Brown. In fact, Mason gives as flawless a performance in this film as he did as the captain in the earlier film version of "The Secret Sharer."

In Alpert's review of *Jim* he goes on to say that Richard Brooks, who had previously brought Scott Fitzgerald and Dostoevsky to the screen, had finally outdone himself by making a superb film adaptation of a great novel. "If the film doesn't have the classic stature of its progenitor," writes Alpert, "it is a beautiful film to watch; and Richard Brooks can now in good conscience claim his place among the important American film makers."[24]

Chapter 7

Blade and Guitar: *The Rover* (1967) and *The Duellists* (1977)

The Rover: The Novel

When Conrad was approaching his twilight years, he opted to pen a novel about a mariner who was likewise in his twilight years, which thus might be called Conrad's own "Rime of the Ancient Mariner."

The story of *The Rover*, set during the Napoleonic Wars, focuses on Peyrol, an aging French pirate who is wanted by the French authorities for capital crimes. A French lieutenant named Réal comes to see him at the inn where he is hiding out and offers him an alternative to the guillotine. The lieutenant says that if Peyrol is willing to allow himself to be captured by an English ship while he is carrying a packet of false dispatches, he can change the course of the war and win a pardon for himself.

The false packet of papers contains a spurious outline of Napoleon's plan for a naval battle to which the emperor's signature has been forged. When the packet is found on Peyrol, the arresting officers will surely relay it immediately to Lord Nelson, the leader of the British fleet, in order to mislead him and his staff about Napoleon's real plans for a naval attack on the British navy.

Peyrol decides that he prefers an English jail to a French guillotine, and so he agrees to carry out the plan of action that the lieutenant has presented to him. Catharine Rising, in her recent Conrad study, indicates that Peyrol has yet another personal motive for taking on the mission he has been offered, besides the one just mentioned: "the desire of a sexagenarian to expire gloriously"—and not to die in bed, as Peyrol himself puts it, "like an old yard dog in his kennel."[1]

He deliverately steers his little skiff into enemy waters where a British man-of-war, the *Amelia,* fires on him before he gets a chance to surrender himself to the enemy. As Conrad describes the scene, "Half a dozen of the *Amelia's* marines stood ranged on the fourcastle-head ready with their muskets." Capt. Vincent "waved his hat and the marines discharged their muskets. Capt. Vincent observed the white-headed man, who was steering, clasp his hand to his left side. . . . The marines on the poop fired in their turn, all the reports merging into one. Voices were heard on the decks crying that they 'had hit the white-hired chap.'" As for Peyrol, "A feeling of peace sank into him, not unmingled with pride. Everything he had planned had come to pass."[2]

Thus Peyrol does not escape death by going along with Lt. Réal's hoax, but gives his life to carry out the plan to deceive the enemy about French naval operations on the eve of the battle of Trafalgar.

Just before his little boat sinks with his corpse lying in its hull, a British officer rows out to it and commandeers the packet of false documents which he in turn relays to Lord Nelson, just as the lieutenant counted on him to do. Hence Peyrol, the scoundrel and pirate, is able to die with the knowledge that he has changed the course of the war and become something of a hero in the bargain.

"Since his piracies have occurred long ago and far away, in Eastern waters," Rising remarks, "Conrad evidently meant him to be judged by his actions at the close of the novel." As a matter of fact, the British admiral himself pays tribute to Peyrol for his heroic death by drawing "a parallel between himself and [Peyrol] as patriots."[3] Nelson muses, "I am like that white-headed man. . . . I will stick to my task till perhaps some shot from the enemy puts an end to everything" (275-76).

Paul Kirschner was cited earlier in this study to the effect that one of Conrad's vividly imagined scenes could easily be transcribed into a film. The death of Peyrol is definitely such a scene, for it is stirringly reproduced in the film version of *The Rover,* as we shall have occasion to note.

As I said in the Introduction of the book, Conrad again and again implies in his fiction that one gains salvation through sacrifice and suffering; and the concept of redemption through personal sacrifice is patent in the final pages of *The Rover*. One sees how Peyrol, a disreputable buccaneer, atones for a life of bloodshed and thievery by going to his death in the service of his country. Nevertheless, the fact that Conrad's thematic vision is apparent in the film version of this novel, just as it is in the novel itself, does not redeem the film from its flaws, some of which we shall now consider.

The Rover: The Film

The film version of *The Rover* boasts an excellent cast, topped by Anthony Quinn *(Zorba the Greek)* as Peyrol and Rita Hayworth *(Gilda)* as Caterina, the keeper of the inn which Peyrol uses as a hideout. In addition, Terrence Young *(From Russia with Love)*, a noteworthy director, was at the helm of the production; so the film seemed to have charted a course for distinction. Unfortunately, the movie turned out to have done nothing of the kind.

It is clear that the studio had little hope that the film would find an audience since it was produced in 1966, but shelved until 1971, when it received a limited release in America. Film historian Gene Ringgold cites William Thomaier, an expert on the Conrad films, as saying that once one had seen the picture, it was easy to see why the studio had no confidence in the finished picture: "The storyline is never lucid; and the tempo is tedious, as Quinn seeks refuge in a seacoast town with Rita Hayworth." On the credit side of the ledger, however, Thomaier adds, "The film's ending, incidentally," in which Quinn "sets sail in a small boat toward his death from the guns of the British warship, is well done." Indeed it is.

When Capt. Vincent (Anthony Dawson) spots Peyrol in his boat, he realizes that this sly old sailor is the man carrying the packet of confidential papers he is seeking. Capt. Vincent opens fire on Peyrol's craft and Peyrol is mortally wounded. The captain then dispatches a long boat to obtain the secret documents Peyrol is carrying, before Peyrol's boat sinks. One of the captain's crew asks him what should be done about the white-haired old man, and the captain replies with the most moving passage of dialogue in the film. "We'll leave him to the waves; a ship makes the best coffin for a sailor, and this was a great sailor." With that, Capt. Vincent salutes Peyrol as his boat drifts farther out to sea.

Ringgold, by the way, describes a sequence at the end of the movie in which Caterina watches a ceremony from the shore "in which Peyrol's body, in the true tradition of a sailor's funeral, is put to sea in a burning boat."[4] To set the record straight, Ringgold's memory has played him false, since the scene as described appears nowhere in the complete print of the film that is in the Library of Congress Film Archive. In addition, Ringgold also states that the film of *The Rover* was based on a posthumous novel of Conrad's when in fact the novel was published a year before Conrad's death in 1924.

The film version of *The Rover* was a financial disaster, and prompted one small town exhibitor to complain to his distributor at the time, "Don't send me no more pictures about people who write with feathers!" Nevertheless, although the film was little seen when it was initially released, *The Rover* (like *An Outcast of the Islands*) has since found a respectable audience on *The Late Show*, where it can be seen as one of the better costume epics of its time.

The Duel: The Novella

Like *The Rover*, "The Duel" is set during the Napoleonic Wars. According to his "Author's Note" in *A Set of Six*, the collection of short fiction in which it appears, the story had its origin in a "ten-line paragraph in a provincial French newspaper." Conrad had run across the item while doing research in a library in France for a novel about the Napoleonic era entitled *Suspense*, which he left unfinished at his death.[5]

The story begins with a statement that Napoleon "disliked duelling between the officers of his army. . . . Nevertheless, a story of duelling, which began a legend in the army, runs through the epic of imperial wars. To the surprise and admiration of their fellows, two officers . . . pursued a private contest through the years of universal carnage" (165).

The novella concerns two cavalry officers in Napoleon's army, Lt. D'Hubert and Lt. Feraud. The latter is an excellent swordsman and enjoys proving his expertise with the blade by challenging his fellow officers to a duel at the least provocation. Conrad writes that Feraud conceived war "as, in the main, a massed lot of personal contacts, a sort of gregarious duelling." Feraud became restless during the interludes of peace which periodically occurred in the course of the Napoleonic Wars. Hence he enjoyed fighting duels during peacetime, since he saw these duels as enabling him to conduct private wars of his own. When Feraud had a duel to fight, says Conrad, "the shadow of peace passed away from him like the shadow of death" (233).

When Feraud has a disagreement with D'Hubert over some minor "point of honor" (the original title of the novella), he challenges D'Hubert to a duel. The precise occasion for the duel comes about in the following manner. D'Hubert is ordered by his commanding officer to find Feraud and inform him that he is to be confined to quarters for defying the emperor's prohibition against duelling. D'Hubert tracks down Feraud in the salon of an aristocratic lady of the town and advises him of his arrest. Feraud responds that D'Hubert has dishonored him by delivering their superior officer's orders about his house arrest while he was talking to a lady, and forthwith challenges D'Hubert to a duel. The contest ends with D'Hubert knocking Feraud to the ground; and Feraud then insists on another encounter, which will afford him a second chance to prove his swordsmanship.

Over a period of fifteen years the two officers meet on the field of honor for a series of confrontations at sword's point, but always with the same outcome: neither ever seems to score a decisive victory over the other, with the frustrating result that they must meet for what appears to be an endless number of encounters. D'Hubert and Feraud are both retired from the army before their last duel. Having returned to his family's estate, D'Hubert falls in love with Adele, a young woman who is several years younger than he. Because of the significant differ-

ence in their ages, D'Hubert is not certain that Adele really
loves him. It is during the period of their engagement that he
fights his final duel with Feraud.

After this fifth and final duel the two men mutually agree to
call it quits. When D'Hubert returns home after the encounter,
he learns that Adele had been a nervous wreck while she was
waiting to find out the outcome of the duel. Adele's display of
anxious concern for him makes D'Hubert finally realize how
deeply she loves him—something he would otherwise not have
known, had he not fought a duel that morning with Feraud. "I
owe it all to that stupid brute. He had made plain in a morning
what might have taken me years to find out," D'Hubert muses
(264).

"Until D'Hubert's sudden exposure to the effects of romantic
love in his own live," Ruth Nadelhaft reflects, "a preoccupation
with traditional heroic values consumes his energies." She continues, "At the climax of the story, however, the love of a young
woman succeeds in separating life from duel as no other
human relationship could have done. D'Hubert realizes,
through the passionate response of his young fiancee, that he
exists as a man, a humane and feeling man, rather than an
exemplar of honor alone."[6]

D'Hubert is so grateful to Feraud for being the occasion of
his discovering the depths of Adele's devotion to him that he
subsequently writes to Feraud, his former enemy, asking that
they now become friends. In passing, D'Hubert mentions his
newborn son, Charles. Feraud responds by declining
D'Hubert's offer of friendship because D'Hubert did not name
his child after Napoleon. To Feraud's mind this fact proves
once again that D'Hubert "*never* loved the emperor" (265). As a
matter of fact, Feraud has always maintained over the years that
the original cause of the duels was that D'Hubert did not love
the emperor (though we know this is not true). In any case, the
fact that D'Hubert, like Feraud himself, had devoted his military
career to waging war on the emperor's behalf never caused the
stubborn, narrow-minded Feraud to waiver in this conviction.

Ironically enough, once their duelling is over for good,
D'Hubert realizes that all the excitement has gone out of his
life. He actually misses the skirmishes with Feraud because each

additional encounter with Feraud was like an "additional pinch of spice in a hot dish. He would never taste it again. It was all over" (223). The ongoing duel with Feraud had given D'Hubert something to look forward to. To some extent "life was robbed of its charm, simply because it was no longer menaced" (259).

The Duellists: The Film

Conrad commented on his *Set of Six* that in composing these stories he had simply tried his best "to be entertaining."[7] It is not surprising, therefore, that film maker Ridley Scott found *The Duel* an entertaining story which he rightly thought would appeal to film viewers. The film, which stars Keith Carradine (*Nashville*) as D'Hubert and Harvey Keitel (*Taxi Driver*) as Feraud, went on to win the prize for the best first film by a new director at the 1977 Cannes Film Festival and thus marked Scott as a director of promise—a promise which has been fulfilled in later films like *Alien*. Scott, by the way, paid homage to Conrad in *Alien* by naming the space ship in that science-fiction film Nostromo.

When making a film Scott, like all major directors, personally supervises every aspect of the film making process. Thus Susan Doll points out, "Scott assumes control over the visual elements of his films as much as possible, rather than turn the set design completely over to the art director or the photography over to the cinematographer. Because his first feature, *The Duellists,* was shot in France, Scott was able to serve as his own cinematographer for that film—a luxury not allowed on many subsequent films due to union rules."[8]

The picture opens with a narrator (Stacey Keach) informing the filmgoer that the film begins in Strasbourg in 1801, the year that Napoleon became emperor of the French and ends in 1815, the year that he was banished to St. Helena. Since *The Duellists* follows the plot of "The Duel" fairly closely, the film goes on to present the initial duel between D'Hubert and Feraud, which ends with Feraud being wounded. Feraud obstinately insists on a return match, and so the pair engage in a second duel six months later. This time D'Hubert is wounded. He is nursed back to health by a camp follower named Flora, who is his mistress (Diana Quick). The episode in which Flora figures represents one of Scott's few additions to the novella's storyline.

Throughout the film Scott shows himself a master of visual imagery, as in the scene in which Flora visits Feraud in his army tent, in an effort to persuade him not to fight another duel with her lover. As she chides him for feeding his spite at D'Hubert's expense, there is a fire smouldering in the center of the tent which symbolizes visually Feraud's burning hostility toward his adversary. Hence he scoffs at her pleas. Flora ultimately decides to leave D'Hubert, since she cannot abide being in love with someone whose life is forever in danger. In fact, she warns him during their last meeting that his next duel will be his last: "This time you'll be killed."

Another meaningful visual symbol occurs in the subsequent scene in which D'Hubert returns to his quarters, only to find that Flora has written "Goodbye" on the blade of his sword in blood-red lipstick. In this way she tells her erstwhile lover that she cannot go on loving a man whose life may end any time in a bloody duel.

Scott said in a television interview at the time of the film's release that he introduced Flora into the film in order to indicate that, as time goes on, D'Hubert becomes so obsessed by his feud with Feraud that he is willing to sacrifice his relationship with Flora in order to continue the never-ending duel. [9]

The third duel takes place in a stable near Austerlitz, after both officers have been promoted to a captaincy. It is painfully clear that the duels are getting increasingly more savage, as the two opponents hack at each other with sabres until they are both exhausted. The setting for the fourth duel is a forest near Lubeck. The comrades of the two opponents insist that this encounter take place on horseback since, after all, both men are cavalry officers. Before this duel begins Scott adroitly inserts a brief fantasy sequence into the scene.

As D'Hubert charges at Feraud, he imagines that he sees Flora repeating her last words to him, "This time you'll be killed." Spurred on by Flora's warning, D'Hubert is determined to preserve his life; and so he flails with his sword at Feraud with great ferocity. After he slashes Feraud across the forehead, the contest cannot continue, and hence they must fight again another day.

Six years later in 1813, D'Hubert and Feraud, who are both colonels by now, meet once again, this time during the ignominious retreat of Napoleon's army from Moscow. As Conrad notes, "The retreat from Moscow submerged all private feelings in a sea of disaster and misery" (211). Consequently, instead of turning their pistols on each other, D'Hubert and Feraud join forces to rout a party of Cossacks. After the skirmish, Feraud says to D'Hubert ominously, "Pistols next time"—instead of the swords they have employed up to now.

By the end of the Napoleonic Wars two years later, both D'Hubert and Feraud have become generals. D'Hubert returns to his country home in Tours, where he falls in love with Adele (Cristina Rains); in due course he proposes to her and she accepts. As they share a kiss, their two white horses, standing behind them, can be seen nuzzling each other. As Pauline Kael says, "This is either the luckiest shot a beginner movie director ever caught or the most entranced bit of planning a beginner ever dared."[10]

At the wedding celebration Adele's father expresses his satisfaction that Napoleon has been defeated once and for all, and encourages D'Hubert to denounce the former emperor. D'Hubert politely declines to do so, thus subtly giving the lie to Feraud's accusation, which echoes throughout the film, that D'Hubert "never loved the emperor."

D'Hubert learns that Feraud is included on a list of political undesireables who have been condemned to be executed before a firing squad because they continue to be rabidly loyal to Napoleon. He therefore goes to Paris to plead with Joseph Fouche, the head of the Paris police (Albert Finney), to strike Feraud's name from the list. Fouche grants D'Hubert's petition, whereupon D'Hubert asks that Feraud never be told who saved his life. By intervening on Feraud's behalf, D'Hubert demonstrates that he no longer harbors any animosity against his former foe.

But Feraud still hates D'Hubert. In fact, when he learns where D'Hubert is living in the country, he dispatches two of his old comrades to offer D'Hubert one last challenge to a duel.

D'Hubert is appalled to learn that he must once more be at the disposal of the malevolent Feraud. Nevertheless, he reluctantly accepts the challenge and agrees to meet Feraud the next morning in a nearby forest for their fifth and final contest. Their weapons are to be pistols, just as Feraud had indicated when they met during the retreat from Moscow. They agree to stalk each other through the woods and fire at will. Once the duel commences, Feraud soon runs out of ammunition. He throws down his empty gun and shouts defiantly at D'Hubert, "Go on and kill me!"

Scott shrewdly increases the suspense of the scene at this point by not portraying immediately the ultimate outcome of the duel. Instead the director shows D'Hubert coming out of the woods alone, as Feraud's two comrades inquire if Feraud is dead. D'Hubert does not answer. Then we see the disconsolate Feraud walking alone in the forest, as we hear D'Hubert saying, voice-over on the sound track, "You have kept me at your beck and call for fifteen years. By all the laws of single combat your life belongs to me. I have submitted to your options of honor long enough. You will now submit to mine. From now on you will live as a dead man to me, whom I never wish to see again." At this point there is a short flashback, showing D'Hubert uttering the last words of his ultimatum to Feraud as he holds his pistol pointed at Feraud's chest.

The film concludes with a final shot of Feraud, wearing an overcoat and three-cornered hat that make him look like Napoleon himself, and gazing at the horizon above the mountains in the distance. Like Napoleon, Feraud is a defeated man who has no place in a France at peace.

In examining the critical response to *The Duellists*, I should like to cite an exchange of letters in *Joseph Conrad Today*, in order to indicate that I am not alone in my admiration of the film. Roderick Davis singled out *The Duellists* as "simply one of the most satisfying adaptations of Conrad to film yet made."[11] William Costanzo observed that Ridley Scott produced a film which "reproduces much of the spirit of the original story."[12] Furthermore, Juliet McLauchlan stated that the movie was in many ways a "brilliantly realized film."[13] This is not to say, however, that the film is perfect. For one thing, Scott's ending for the movie differs from that of the novella, and not for the better. In "The Duel," we recall, it is only when D'Hubert learns that Adele was virtually hysterical with worry about him as she awaited news of the outcome of the duel that he is genuinely assured for the first time of her deep attachment to him. D'Hubert further realizes that he owes this discovery to Feraud, who had challenged him to the duel. Consequently, D'Hubert winds up feeling grateful to a man whom he had hated all his life. This ironic dimension to the ending of the novella is missing from the film. Hence the film's ending to that extent suffers by comparison with that of the novella.

A second reservation about the film is that it should have devoted more time to examining the psychology of character. For example, Scott fails to depict the character of D'Hubert in any depth. As Davis notes in *Literature/Film Quarterly*, D'Hubert is so stoically loyal to the demands that the ongoing duel have made on his code of honor as an officer and a gentleman, that the full scope of the horror with which the ongoing duel persistently shadows his life "never seems quite to register with the impact that it should."[14] Thus, when D'Hubert is challenged to the final duel, he must feel somewhat frightened by the fact that the duel may end his joyous relationship with Adele by putting an end to his life; but Scott never depicts for us D'Hubert's feelings in the matter to any significant degree.

Conversely, at the point in the story at which D'Hubert is challenged to the last duel, Conrad makes it abundantly clear that the prospect of meeting his death and thereby losing Adele fills D'Hubert with melancholy despair. Indeed, he has never felt himself the prisoner of Feraud's obsession more than at this moment. The character of Feraud is likewise not portrayed in any depth in the film, although we do get hints at times of what drives his hostility toward D'Hubert. For example, Feraud harbors for D'Hubert the hatred of a commoner for an aristocrat. Hence Feraud's outrage at the insult he fancied that D'Hubert visited upon him the first time they met was fueled by the fact that Feraud felt that a commoner was being put down by one of his social "betters"; and he simply could not tolerate that.

Nevertheless, Feraud still comes across for the most part as a one-dimensional character, possessing only one central drive, which Pauline Kael identifies as implacability. He has a single-minded hatred for D'Hubert that compels him to want to duel with D'Hubert endlessly.

In short, Scott could have spent more screen time on character development. To be more specific, the plot of the film goes into overdrive before the viewer gets a chance to become intimately acquainted with the principals, and consequently to understand their conflicts, to the same extent that one can do in Reed's excellent adaptation of *An Outcast of the Islands*. On the other hand, because *Outcast* devotes more of its running time to character development, something that is somewhat lacking to the same degree in *The Duellists*, the Reed film contains a few slow-paced, talky stretches that sometimes cause the filmgoer's interest to flag—something which never happens in *The Duellists*.

In the last analysis, whether one prefers a fast-paced action film with a minimum of character development, like *The Duellists*, to a longer, somewhat denser film that reflects a deeper probing into the psychology of character, as in *An Outcast of the Islands*, says more about one's personal cinematic taste than it does about the films in question.

Chapter 8

Darkness at Noon:
Heart of the Forest (1979)
and *Apocalypse Now* (1979)

Heart of Darkness: The Novella

In *A Personal Record* Conrad recalls that in 1868, as a boy of nine, he looked at a map of Africa, placed his finger on one of the uncharted areas of the continent, and said to himself, "When I grow up, I shall go *there*."[1] And, as things turned out, when he grew up he did go *there*. By then the region was known as Stanley Falls. His reason for journeying to the African continent in the summer of 1890 was that a Belgian trading firm had offered him the command of a steamer that would transport men and materials between the trading posts that the company maintained along the coast of the Congo River.

When Conrad arrived in Africa, however, a representative of the trading company by which he was employed eventually informed him that promises made by officials of the firm in Europe carried no weight in the trading company's posts in Africa, unless they were in writing. The promises made to Conrad were not. The upshot was that there was no permanent command awaiting Conrad as a naval officer in the Congo; and he accordingly had no choice but to return to Europe to seek employment with another shipping firm there—he had at this point in time not as yet decided to devote himself full-time to being a writer. He was back in London by February, 1891. Still the short time Conrad spent in Africa was enough to allow him to produce a short *Congo Diary*, a brief record of his experiences there, and to inspire him to compose one of his greatest stories, "Heart of Darkness."

While sojourning in Africa, waiting for a command that never materialized, Conrad made a trip up the Congo River on a small steamer called the *King of the Belgians* to pick up a Frenchman named Georges Antoine Klein, an agent of the trading company under whose auspices Conrad had gone to Africa in the first place. Klein had become gravely ill with some tropical disease while serving at one of the company's outposts along the Congo River; hence he was slated to return to Europe where he could receive more adequate medical care. Conrad and his fellow seamen picked up Klein at Stanley Falls; but Klein did not survive the return trip aboard the *King of the Belgians,* and hence was never to return to Europe.

Conrad had originally called the villain of "Heart of Darkness" Klein (which means *small* in German); but he eventually changed the character's name to Kurtz (which means *short* in German), possibly to dissociate Klein from the evil Kurtz of the novella, one of the vilest human beings that Conrad ever conceived.

"Heart of Darkness," the novella which Conrad mined from his Congo experience, is narrated by a mariner named Marlow, who also narrated *Lord Jim.* He is charged by the trading company by which he is employed in the Congo with investigating the disappearance of Kurtz, an ivory trader employed by the same company. Marlow must track down Kurtz in the interior of the African jungle in which he has disappeared. Sometime earlier Kurtz had sailed up the Congo to manage one of the firm's trading posts, but never returned. Rumors had circulated from one post to another that Kurtz (like Klein) had fallen ill with some tropical disease. Accordingly Marlow is given command of a small steamer to sail up the Congo, find Kurtz, and bring him back to the central trading post, where he can be dispatched back to Europe for better medical attention.

Gradually Marlow unearths the known facts about what has happened to Kurtz by inquiring about him en route from other traders who have known him. Marlow narrates his journey in a series of flashbacks. The events of Kurtz's life are revealed to Marlow in the course of his voyage up the Congo River by a number of witnesses, none of whom knows the whole story about Kurtz; and Marlow, in turn, puts together the hideous facts about Kurtz as they are brought to light.

It seems that when Kurtz first came to the Congo he saw himself as a kind of missionary who wanted to civilize the natives he dealt with at his trading post in the jungle, and not merely bargain with them for the precious stores of ivory that they had accumulated in the bush. But Kurtz was not equipped with the kind of deep moral convictions that would sustain him when he faced the challenges of the wilderness on his own. Thus Conrad suggests that, if someone like Kurtz lacks strong ethical principles of his own, the superficial restraints which civilized society places on one's moral behavior, represented by the guardians of Law and Order, are gradually forgotten in the isolated, barbaric atmosphere of the wilderness. In essence, the jungle is depicted in "Heart of Darkness" as a metaphor for the heart of darkness which lies in each of us; i.e., the inclination to evil that lurks within each of us.

To be more specific about Kurtz's case, the heart of darkness within Kurtz manifested itself once he began running his own trading post singlehandedly in the heart of the jungle; for he gradually became guilty of the most appalling behavior. As Gurko puts it in his book on Conrad, Kurtz lost his footing and plunged into an abyss of moral degradation. He became a ruthless, greedy despot, who exploited the natives, even to the extent of employing violence in order to extort from them as much ivory as he could. Indeed, Marlow comments that Kurtz "had collected, bartered, swindled, or stolen more ivory" than all of the other agents of the trading company put together.[2]

Furthermore, Kurtz allowed the tribesmen to worship him as a demi-god, and in this manner he kept them subservient to him. Kurtz accordingly engaged with the tribesmen in the most barbaric pagan rites, which were offered in his own honor. In Marlow's words, Kurtz willingly presided "at certain midnight dances ending with unspeakable rites, which—as far as I reluctantly gathered from what I heard at various times—were offered up to him . . . to Mr. Kurtz himself" (118).

When Marlow and his party approach Kurtz's compound in their steamer, the natives attack the boat with a shower of arrows and spears at Kurtz's behest, in an attempt to keep the interlopers from taking away their adored leader. Once Marlow and his men ward off the attack and enter Kurtz's domain, Marlow begins to examine the area.

He focuses his spyglass on Kurtz's house, which is surrounded by a fence. Marlow is appalled to discover, as he peers through his spyglass, a row of shrunken heads impaled on the fence posts. He gazes at one of the grotesque heads, as it appears up-close in his spyglass—as if it were a close-up in a film: "There it was, black, dried, sunken, with closed eyelids—a head that seemed to sleep at the top of that pole, and, with shrunken dry lips showing a narrow white line of the teeth" (130-31). These heads, it seems, belonged to renegade tribesmen, who had dared to rebel against Kurtz's tyranny. In sum, Kurtz has enslaved the natives over whom he holds sway as demi-god. Thus, writes Carl Bennett, this first glimpse of Kurtz's compound allows Marlow to plumb "in anticipation . . . the dark depths of Kurtz's soul."[3]

After Marlow at last encounters the deathly ill Kurtz, he places him in a cabin aboard the steamer which is docked at the river bank, in preparation for the return trip down river to the trading company's central station. Shortly afterward, Marlow discovers that Kurtz has disappeared from the boat, and has gone to participate in one of the barbarous rituals held in his honor. Marlow follows the trail through the grass which Kurtz has left behind him, and is able to discover by these tracks that Kurtz, in his weakened condition, cannot walk. "He's crawling on all fours—I've got him," Marlow exclaims (142). Kurtz is reduced to crawling along the ground like the animal he has become; for his savage behavior has reduced him to the level of a brute beast.

When Marlow catches up with him, Kurtz manages to stand upright to confront his pursuer. At this moment, says Stephen Land, we have reached the climax of the story, wherein Marlow earnestly strives to persuade Kurtz to abandon his morally corrupt way of life and return to Europe with him.

Not very far away from where they stand, the diabolical pagan rites which Kurtz aims to attend are already in progress. Marlow can discern a fiendish witch doctor looming near the fires that provide light for the ceremony. Marlow begs Kurtz to forsake such pagan practices once and for all and return to civilization with him. Marlow whispers, "Do you know what you are doing?" Kurtz replies laconically, "Perfectly." He obviously intends to stay on in the jungle, enacting the role of demi-god for his tribesmen, for as long as his fragile life shall last. "You will be lost," Marlow says ruefully, "utterly lost."

But Marlow believes that it is already too late to save Kurtz from himself and his evil inclinations. "Indeed," Marlow reflects, "he could not be more irretrievably lost" than he is at this moment (143). For it is the heart of darkness within Kurtz that has driven him on this night "to the edge of the forest, toward the gleam of fires, the throb of drums, the drone of weird incantations." Hence, Marlow concludes, he is dealing with a being to whom he cannot appeal "in the name of anything high or low," since Kurtz no longer recognizes as valid the moral principles to which he had once subscribed (144). Marlow realizes, then, that, as far as he can judge, Kurtz is a lost soul; and he consequently declines to argue with him any longer. Instead, he picks up the ailing man and carries him back to the steamer for the trip back to Europe—a journey which Kurtz will not survive. In fact, Kurtz expires aboard the steamer with the cryptic words on his lips, "The horror, the horror" (149).

Presumably Kurtz's repetition of the phrase "the horror" when he was on the point of death reflects that, before he succumbed to the deadly tropical disease that took his life, he got a flash of personal insight into his life that forced him to see the hideous horror of his moral corruption. That is to say, in his steady moral disintegration he had finally become more savage than any of the savages he had initially wanted to civilize. Or, in the words of Andrew Gillon in his volume on Conrad, "Kurtz's cry represents a revulsion against his darker self, a sign that he was not completely lost."[4]

When Marlow returns home, he goes to see Kurtz's fiancée, who has remained faithful to Kurtz, despite his prolonged sojourn in the Congo. Marlow gently tells her of Kurtz's demise. With supreme irony Marlow reassures her that "his end . . . was in every way worthy of his life" (161). When she asks him what her fiancé's last words were, Marlow cannot bring himself to inform her that Kurtz's final painful utterance was "the horror, the horror." He rather tells her that Kurtz died speaking her name. Marlow, after all, does not wish to destroy her fond memories of her deceased fiancé, which are all she has left of him.

As Catharine Rising writes, Marlow's lie preserves the young woman's "deluded love of the dead. To suppress Kurtz's actual words . . . signifies not only Marlow's compassion," but his admiration for a woman "who strikes him as beautiful, and in whom . . . he lauds a mature capacity for fidelity" to her beloved.[5]

Among Kurtz's private papers Marlow comes across a report which Kurtz had composed during his early days in Africa, which he had addressed to the International Society for the Suppression of Savage Customs. In it Kurtz maintains that the white man, in his desire to civilize the native population, "can exert a power for good practically unbounded" on the Africans. Marlow finds a postscript, however, which was evidently appended to the manuscript much later. It is scrawled in an unsteady hand across the last page of the report: "Exterminate the brutes" (118). Kurtz's final statement implies the contempt which he ultimately felt, in the depths of his moral disintegration, for the natives he had initially wanted to civilize.

Richard Ambrosini notes that Marlow begins his tale by stating that he wants to recount the events of his story in order that his audience can understand the effect of the events on himself. In other words, Marlow wants to share with his audience what Ambrosini terms "the self-knowledge he has acquired during the voyage."[6]

More specifically, Gillon observes that Marlow emerges from his encounter with Kurtz in the wilderness a wiser if sadder man.[7] Marlow thus learns from Kurtz's moral deterioration that one can only cope with one's personal capacity for evil by recognizing it for what it is. In sum, Conrad portrays human nature in the novella with a potential for greatness, which is coupled with an inclination toward evil that can finally undermine that capacity for good—which is precisely what happened to Kurtz.

Heart of Darkness: The Orson Welles Scenario

The first attempt to bring "Heart of Darkness" to the screen was made by Orson Welles *(Citizen Kane)*, who had originally hoped that his film adaptation of Conrad's story would be the first film he made in Hollywood for RKO, the studio with which he signed a contract in 1939. Welles wanted to begin shooting the film in the fall of 1939 (he had planned to be the voice of Marlow, the narrator of the story, voice-over on the sound track as well as to appear on-screen as Kurtz). Unfortunately neither the script nor the budget of the film were ready at that point. When Welles finally turned in his proposed budget for the production, it ran to more than one million dollars—much to the dismay of RKO's front office since that was exactly twice the budget for the average RKO film. The studio brass accordingly insisted that Welles cut his budget in half, and he responded that he would do his best to be obliging.

The draft of Welles's screenplay for "Heart of Darkness" was literally taken from the source story. As a matter of fact, Robert Carringer notes in his book on Welles that Welles actually tore pages of the story out of the paperback edition of the novella "and pasted them onto sheets of typing paper; and he worked his way through these, marking the passages that were to be retained and crossing out the rest." Occasionally, however, Welles "changed or added a line or two," and made other alterations in the screenplay. Thus he updated the story to the present and made Marlow, the film's narrator, an American; but Welles maintained that whatever changes he made in the original story Conrad himself would have desired, were he alive at the time the film was being made.

Unfortunately plans to film *Heart of Darkness* were finally abandoned by the studio when it became obvious that *Heart of Darkness,* with its elaborate jungle sets and "casts of thousands," could never be made for $500,000. In fact, Welles's script called for three thousand black natives to be seen bowing down to Kurtz in one sequence which caused one dismayed RKO executive to point out to the front office that there were only four or five hundred black extras in all of Hollywood.[8] Undaunted,

Welles then turned his attention to making *Citizen Kane;* and the rest, as they say, is history.

Heart of the Forest: Manuel Aragon's Version of Heart of Darkness

Interestingly enough, the Spanish film maker Manuel Aragon had the world premiere of his adaptation of "Heart of Darkness," entitled *Heart of the Forest,* at the Berlin Film Festival the same spring of 1979 in which Coppola unveiled his version of Heart of Darkness entitled *Apocalypse Now* at Cannes.

Aragon's film takes place in the period following the Spanish Civil War. As the story unfolds, Andarin (Luis Politti), the Kurtz character in *Heart of the Forest,* has steadfastly refused to admit that the Civil War is over and that the anti-fascist side on which he fought has lost the war to Franco and his fascists. Andarin uses guerrilla tactics to go on fighting his own private war in the wilderness against Franco's fascist regime which came to power at the end of the Civil War.

Juan (Norman Briski), the Marlow character in *Heart of the Forest,* has continued to look up to Andarin in the period following the war as one of the great anti-fascist heroes of the Civil War. He very much wants to meet the man he so much admires; and so he tracks Andarin down in his wilderness retreat. When Juan finally locates Andarin's stronghold in the forest, he finds that Andarin is deathly ill. Aware that the fascist military police are still hunting for Andarin, Juan comes to believe that the guerrilla leader would rather meet death bravely, at the hands of someone who admires him as Juan does, rather than be ignominiously executed by the military police as a ragged renegade.

Andarin too understands the situation in this fashion and so he allows Juan to shoot him and then bury him in a hero's grave in his compound in the forest. Moreover, Juan reasons that in death Andarin will continue to be an abiding inspiration to the anti-fascist cause. One big difference, of course, between "Heart of Darkness" and *Heart of the Forest* is that the Kurtz character in the novella is fundamentally an evil man, while the Kurtz character in *Forest* is essentially a good man. Another difference between book and film is that Aragon updated the story to the period following the Spanish Civil War (just as Coppola, as we shall soon see, updated his film to the Vietnam War).

Film critic Luis Guarnez praised Aragon's movie, finding it to be the finest film directed by Manuel Gutierrez Aragon.[9] By contrast, *Variety* in its review of *Heart of the Forest* (March 21, 1979), dismissed Aragon's direction of the film as florid and pretentious. I tend to agree with *Variety*'s cool reception of the film; for *Heart of the Forest* is really a bargain basement version of *Apocalypse Now* because it is simply not in the same class with Coppola's masterwork.

Apocalypse Now: Francis Coppola's Version of Heart of Darkness

In the spring of 1975 the distinguished American director Francis Coppola *(The Godfather)* told an interviewer that his next film would deal with the Vietnam War. As a starting point for his screenplay Coppola noted that he had selected a six-year-old scenario done by writer-director John Milius *(The Wind and the Lion)* in 1969, based on Conrad's "Heart of Darkness." The script had updated the story to the Vietnam War and turned Kurtz from an ivory trader into a Green Beret officer who defects from the American army and sets up his own army across the Cambodian border where he proceeds to conduct his own private war against the Vietcong.

When Milius initially discussed with Coppola writing the screenplay of *Apocalypse Now* back in the late 1960's, Coppola suggested to Milius that he use the search for the mysterious Kurtz which provides the fundamental structure of "Heart of Darkness," as the basis for his script. The original plan was that the film would be shot in 16 millimeter, in the style of a documentary, with George Lucas *(Star Wars)* directing and Coppola producing. Nothing came of the project at that time, but six years later Coppola decided to revive it and direct the film himself. Milius revised his original script at this point, after consulting with Coppola; and Coppola, in turn, substantially reshaped Milius's revised screenplay according to his own conception of the story.

In asking the Pentagon in May, 1979, for its co-operation in making the film, Coppola pointed out that the initial script still needed considerable revision. But, as Lawrence Suid states in his article on *Apocalypse Now* in *Film Comment,* the Army, after studying Coppola's scenario, found little basis to discuss the screenplay with Coppola further. What's more, Army officials "pointed to 'several objectionable episodes,'" starting with the film's springboard incident, which has Captain Benjamin Willard sent to assassinate the crazed, power-mad Col. Kurtz.[10] The army said that in an actual situation Willard would be directed to bring Kurtz back for medical treatment rather than ordered to summarily kill Kurtz. Suffice it to say that, when Coppola made no effort whatever to revise his screenplay according to army specifications, the Pentagon advised him that he would not even receive limited cooperation from the Army in the making of the film.

After examining Milius's first-draft script for *Apocalypse Now* (dated December 5, 1969), film scholar Brooks Riley points out in *Film Comment* that Coppola stuck very close to Milius's original scenario when he revised it for production six years later. If the revised script "strayed from the first draft," she writes, "*it was not so much away from Milius's conception*" of the plot "*as toward Milius's source, the Conrad novel.*"[11] (Emphasis added.) In fact, Jeffrey Chown, in his 1988 book on Coppola, cites the director as claiming that at one point he had seriously considered changing the film's title to that of the novella. Little wonder, as film scholar Diane Jacobs says, *Heart of Darkness* is the spine of *Apocalypse Now.*

Brooks Riley notes two major alterations which Coppola made in Milius's version of the script which are particularly significant. One change that Coppola made concerned the very beginning of the screenplay. Milius begins his script with a scene set in Kurtz's stronghold in the jungle, from which his rebel band makes its forays into the jungle against the Vietcong; and in this scene there is a glimpse of Kurtz himself, exhorting his disciples. By contrast, Coppola chose to follow Conrad in this matter by withholding our first sight of Kurtz until Willard finally tracks him down late in the film. Kurtz's absence from the film throughout most of its running time steadily builds suspense in the viewer who continually wonders what this strange and mysterious individual will really be like, once he finally makes his appearance. "To have shown Kurtz first, only to have abandoned him for the next two-thirds of the film," Riley explains, would have proved to be "a dilution of the film's carefully planned unveiling of the man."[12]

The other crucial revision which Coppola made in Milius's screenplay concerned the film's conclusion. In Milius's conception of the film's finale, Willard is so mesmerized by the overpowering personality of Col. Kurtz that he succumbs to the corrupting influence of this barbarous war lord. That is, Willard decides to join the native Cambodian tribesmen and the runaway American soldiers who comprise Kurtz's army. Shortly afterwards, the Vietcong attack Kurtz's compound; and Kurtz and Willard fight side-by-side until Kurtz is killed in battle. American helicopters, which are coming to rescue Willard, then appear in the sky over the compound; and Willard shoots wildly at them, as the film comes to an end.

Coppola was thoroughly dissatisfied with Milius's ending for the film. As Coppola describes this ending, Kurtz, "a battle-mad commander," wearing two bands of machine gun bullets across his chest, takes Willard by the hand and leads him into battle against the North Vietnamese.[13] Elsewhere he adds that thus "Willard converts to Kurtz's side; in the end he's firing up at the helicopters that are coming to get him, crying out crazily."[14]

Needless to say, this finale of the film, as conceived by Milius, departs to a greater degree from Conrad's ending to the story than Coppola's ending for the film does. In Coppola's film Willard recoils from Kurtz's savage practices in the same manner that Marlow does in the book. Hence neither Marlow nor the film's Willard fall under Kurtz's sway in the way that Milius's Willard does.

For the record, *Heart of Darkness* does not appear in the screen credits of *Apocalypse Now* as the literary source of the film. As a matter of fact, a reference to Conrad's novella was originally listed in the screen credits, but was removed when one of the three writers named in the credits as authors of the script complained to the Screen Writers' Guild, and the refer-

ence to the book was removed. The three screenwriters in question are John Milius, Coppola, and Michael Herr, a former war
correspondent in Vietnam who wrote Willard's narration. It is
generally thought in film circles that it was Milius who vetoed
the presence of Conrad's novella in the film's credits, because
he felt that citing Conrad's book as the source of the movie
would minimize the importance of the material contributed to
the screenplay by himself and his co-scripters.

That Milius had for a long time denied the link between
Apocalypse Now and *Heart of Darkness* is borne out in a remark
he made in 1982. At that time Milius had said that, if *Apocalypse
Now* "is based on *Heart of Darkness,* then *Moby Dick* is based on
the book of Job." But a few years later Milius had definitely
changed his mind. In Peter Cowie's book on Coppola, Milius
freely conceded that *Heart of Darkness* is indeed the source story
for the film. "It was my favorite Conrad book," he said; and
hence he wanted very much to bring it to the screen.[15]

When I asked Coppola if I was correct in assuming that it was
Milius who kept Conrad from being in the screen credits of
Apocalypse at the time that the credits were drawn up—even
though he felt differently about the matter afterward—Coppola
declined to answer.

On the surface it seems that Conrad's novella is very different from Coppola's film. For instance, Conrad's story takes
place in the Belgian Congo in the 1890s and focuses on Charles
Marlow, a British sailor employed by a European trading firm
as captain of one of their steamboats. By contrast, Coppola's
film is set in Southeast Asia in the 1960s, and centers on Benjamin Willard, an American army officer. Yet, as film scholar
Linda Cahir points out, although the settings and backgrounds
of novella and film are quite different, the manner in which the
story is narrated in each instance is "splendidly similar." Here is
a brief summary of the fundamental parallels between book and
film.

For example, "each tale-proper begins with the protagonist's
explanation of how he got the appointment which necessitated
his excursion up river," Cahir points out. Marlow is dispatched
to steam up the Congo in order to find Mr. Kurtz, an ivory
trader who disappeared into the interior and never returned.

Willard is mandated to journey up the Mekong River in a navy patrol boat to find Col. Kurtz, who has recruited his own rene-gade army to fight the Vietcong. In addition, while Marlow and Willard each travel up a primeval river to fulfill their respective assignments, each speculates about the character of the man he is seeking, with the help of the information each has pieced together about him. Furthermore, the last stop for both Marlow and Willard, concludes Cahir, "is the soul-altering confronta-tion with the mysterious Kurtz."[16]

Moreover, one of the elements of Coppola's film which serves to bring it closer to the original story is employing Willard as the narrator of the film, just as Marlow is the narra-tor of the novella. Hence the screenplay of *Apocalypse Now* remains most faithful to its source in its attempt to depict the action through flashback, with the narrator's comments on the action heard, voice-over, on the sound track. Hence Willard is what Avrom Fleishman calls in his book *Narrated Films* (already cited) an internal (subjective) narrator, because Willard gives his personal reactions to his own experiences as he narrates them over the soundtrack. By contrast, an external (objective) narrator, like the one in *Laughing Anne*, is so called precisely because he simply reports an objective version of the facts of someone else's life, i.e., that of the title character, Laughing Anne.

As I mentioned at the outset of this book, it is more difficult to imply in a movie, than it is in a work of fiction, that a given account of past events is being presented from the subjective point of view of one of the characters—as when Willard recalls in his voice-over commentary his initial misgivings about carry-ing out his secret orders to assassinate Kurtz when he finds him. This is because a film audience is always conscious that it is watching what is being dramatized in flashback on the screen—*not* through the eyes of the character who is narrating the events in question—but through the eyes of the camera. The screenplay may try to retain the subjective dimension of these memories by having the voice of the character who is recalling the event in question surface on the sound track occasionally to give his subjective reflections on the flashback as it unfolds on the screen, as is the case in the present film. But the viewer still does not have the sense that he is seeing the flashback from the point of view of the character who is retelling the event. By the same token, while the filmgoer is watching *Lord Jim*, he often forgets that he is supposedly seeing Jim's story through the eyes of Marlow, who narrates that film over the sound track as an external (objective) narrator, in Fleishman's sense of that term.

"One cannot tell a story from the single point of view of one character in a film as one can in a novel," Graham Greene once explained. "You cannot look through the eyes of one character in a film." It is true that the central character remains on the screen more than anyone else in the movie, Greene continued, and his comments are often there on the sound track. "But we still don't see others completely from his point of view, as we do in the novel."[17]

Therefore *Apocalypse Now* is robbed of some of the emotional intensity that one feels when one reads "Heart of Darkness," simply because in the book the narrator frequently communicates to the reader his subjective reaction to the episodes from the past he is narrating. For example, the filmgoer never grasps the extent to which Willard, the narrator of the film, is profoundly touched by Kurtz's tragedy in the movie, since many of the sage reflections about Kurtz's life and death which Marlow makes in the book are simply not in the film.

Apocalypse Now, when it finally reached the screen in 1979, turned out to be a mammoth spectacle, which Coppola shot almost entirely on location in the Philippines. As mentioned, the setting of the story is updated from the late Nineteenth Century to the time of the Vietnam War. As we know, Captain Benjamin Willard, played by Martin Sheen *(The Subject was Roses)*, who is the central character and narrator of the movie, is ordered by his superior officers to penetrate into the interior of the jungle and track down Col. Walter E. Kurtz (Marlon Brando), a renegade officer who has raised an army composed of deserters like himself and of native tribesmen, in order to fight the war on his own terms. When he locates Kurtz, Willard is to "terminate his command with extreme prejudice," which is military jargon meaning that Willard should assassinate Kurtz. Col. Kurtz, it seems, rules over his followers like a fanatical war lord, and has taken to employing brutal tactics to attain his objectives; indeed, some of the atrocities Kurtz has committed have sickened the members of the Army intelligence staff who have succeeded in obtaining information about him.

Willard's first reaction to his mission is that liquidating someone for killing people in wartime seems like "handing out speeding tickets at the 'Indy 500.'" Besides, even though Willard has been ordered to eliminate no less than six other Vietnamese political undesirables in the recent past, this is the first time his target has been an American and an officer. He therefore decides to withhold judgment about Kurtz until he meets up with him personally.

As Willard chugs up the Mekong River in a river patrol boat in search of Kurtz, film scholar Richard Blake comments, his journey becomes a symbolic voyage "backward in time." Near the beginning of the trip Willard and the crew of his small craft witness an air attack on a North Vietnamese village carried out by Lieutenant Colonel Kilgore (Robert Duvall), which utilizes all the facilities of modern mechanized warfare, from helicopters and rockets to radar-directed machine guns. By the time that Willard's boat reaches Kurtz's compound in the heart of the dark jungle, the modern weaponry has been replaced by the weapons of primitive man, as Kurtz's native followers, wearing war paint, attack Willard's small vessel with arrows and spears in an attempt to scare off the intruders. (The attack of the natives is taken directly from the novel.) In entering Kurtz's outpost in the wilderness, Willard has equivalently stepped back into a lawless, prehistoric age where barbarism holds sway. The compound, then, becomes a graphic visual metaphor which reflects Kurtz's gradual descent into primitive barbarism.

In fact, the severed heads that lie scattered around the grounds testify to the depths of pagan savagery to which Kurtz has sunk during his sojourn in the jungle. The severed heads, shown in long shot, recall the scene in the novel when Marlow is shocked to see that Kurtz has shrunken heads stuck on pikes in front of his lodgings.

Furthermore, it is painfully clear to Willard that, despite the fact that Kurtz's native followers revere him as a god, Kurtz is incurably insane. Willard also discovers, when he at last meets

Kurtz, that Kurtz is slowly dying of malaria; hence his physical illness is symbolic of his moral sickness.

When Kurtz takes Willard into custody, he is aware of the object of Willard's mission. "You are an errand boy," Kurtz scoffs, "sent by grocery clerks to collect the bill." Then Kurtz, in his malarial delirium, spends hours rambling to Willard about his theories of war and politics, which he maintains lie behind his becoming a rebel chieftain. Kurtz does this, not only because he wants a brother officer to hear his side of the story, but also because he ultimately wants Willard to explain to Kurtz's son his father's reasons for acting as he has. Significantly, even in the depths of his madness, Kurtz has not lost sight of the preciousness of family attachments. (Kurtz is not married in the novella, so Marlow goes to comfort Kurtz's fiancée, not his son, in the book, once he gets to Europe.)

In Kurtz's own mind, the ruthless tactics he has employed to prosecute his own private war represent in essence his unshakable conviction that the only way to conquer a cruel and inhuman enemy like the Vietcong is to become as cruel and inhuman as they are, and crush them by their own hideous methods.

By now Willard has definitely made up his mind to carry out his orders by killing Kurtz; and Kurtz, who has sensed from the beginning the reason why Willard was sent to find him, finally makes no effort to stop him. For one thing, Kurtz presumably prefers a quick death, as meted out by Willard, to a slow death from malaria. More importantly, as Willard explains in his voice-over commentary on the sound track, Kurtz wants to die bravely, like a soldier, at the hands of another soldier, and not be ignominiously butchered as a wretched renegade. Indeed, in order to die like a soldier, Kurtz dons his Green Beret uniform, while he is waiting for Willard to come and assassinate him. Willard accordingly enters Kurtz's murky lair and ceremoniously slays him with a machete. (Kurtz dies of natural causes in the book.)

Willard's killing of Kurtz is intercut with shots of the Cambodian tribe that is part of Kurtz's army slaughtering a sacrificial water buffalo, a scene which suggests that Willard implicitly sees his "execution" of the diabolical Kurtz for his hideous war crimes as a kind of ritual slaying. The ritual killing of the water buffalo, moreover, recalls an earlier sequence, set in Saigon, in which roast beef is served at a dinner, during which a general commissions Willard to assassinate Kurtz: "Fleshy roast beef is aggressively stabbed and cut" during the meal, writes Cahir in describing the scene.[18] The stabbing of the roast beef, film scholar Louis Greiff observes, foreshadows the hacking up of the sacrificial water buffalo, which, in turn, parallels Willard's stabbing Kurtz to death with a machete.[19]

After Willard has slain Kurtz, he pauses at Kurtz's desk and notices a typescript lying on it. We see in close-up that, scrawled in red across one page is the statement, "Drop the Bomb. Exterminate them all!" This is Kurtz's manner of indicating his way of ending the Vietnam War: he would like to have seen all of the North Vietnamese, soldiers and non-combatants alike, destroyed from the air. Col. Kurtz's cold-blooded remark recalls a similar passage in the novella, in which Marlow peruses a report which Kurtz had prepared for the International Society for the Suppression of Savage Customs. The report ends with a postscript, presumably added much later: "Exterminate the brutes."

When Willard leaves Kurtz's quarters, Kurtz's tribesmen submissively lay their weapons on the ground as he passes among them. Clearly they believe that the mantle of authority has passed from their deceased leader to the man he has allowed to slay him. But Willard, his mission accomplished, walks out of the compound and proceeds to the river bank, where his patrol boat awaits him to take him back to civilization.

As the boat pulls away from the shore, Willard hears the voice of Kurtz uttering the same phrase he had spoken just before he met his Maker: "The horror, the horror." At the end Kurtz was apparently vouchsafed a moment of lucidity, in which he realized what a depraved brute he had become. To Willard the phrase represents, as it does to Marlow in the novella, his own revulsion at the vicious inclination to evil he had seen revealed in Kurtz—a tendency that Kurtz had allowed to overpower his better nature and render him more savage by far than the enemy he was so intent on exterminating.

Hence the theme of the movie is the same as that of Conrad's novel. "In *Apocalypse Now,* just as in 'Heart of Darkness,' the central journey is both a literal and a metaphoric one," writes Joy Gould Boyum; it is fundamentally "a voyage of discovery into the dark heart of man, and an encounter with his capacity for evil."[20] In harmony with this observation, Coppola says that he too sees Willard's journey upriver as a metaphor for "the voyage of life that each of us takes within ourselves and during which we choose between good and evil."[21]

Although some critics found those scenes in which Kurtz theorizes about the motivation for his unspeakable behavior wordy and overlong, most agreed that the movie contains some of the most extraordinary combat footage ever filmed. The battle scene that particularly stands out is the one in which the officer who is aptly named Kilgore systematically wipes out a strongly fortified enemy village from the air.

Kilgore, all decked out with a stetson and gold neckerchief, looks as if he should be leading a cavalry charge rather than a helicopter attack. His fleet of helicopters is equipped with loudspeakers that blare forth Wagner's thunderous "Ride of the Valkyries" as the choppers fly over the target area. "Wagner scares the hell out of the natives," Kilgore tells Willard, who is observing the operation as a passenger in Kilgore's copter. As a napalm strike wreaks havoc and destruction on the village below, Kilgore exults, "I love the smell of napalm in the morning. It has the smell of victory." It is spectacular scenes like this one that have prompted some commentators on the film to rank *Apocalypse Now,* which won one of the two Grand Prizes awarded at the 1979 Cannes Film Festival, among the great war movies of all time. Moreover, this writer feels that the film can likewise be numbered among the major adaptations of Conrad to the screen.

Heart of Darkness: Nicholas Roeg's Television Version

A third version of "Heart of Darkness" has reached the screen—albeit the small screen. A made-for-cable version premiered on TNT on March 13, 1994. The television adaptation is significant for sticking to Conrad's period setting, whereas

Heart of the Forest and *Apocalypse Now* updated the story to the Spanish Civil War and the Vietnam War, respectively.

Asked what he thought the theme of the story is, John Malcovich, who plays Kurtz in the telemovie, replied that the TV adaptation of "Heart of Darkness," like its literary source, is "about man's subconscious; it's about how shallow all our cultural and social instincts are."[22] His observation is in complete harmony with the thematic implications of the novella as I have developed them earlier in this chapter. This is another way of saying that the cable version of "Heart of Darkness" is faithful to the spirit of the Conrad original to that extent.

Otherwise the telefilm is not particularly noteworthy. In fact, the critics' assessments of the telemovie were essentially polite but reserved, although most of them singled out Malkovich and Tim Roth (as Marlow) as turning in fine performances. Perhaps the strongest endorsement for the cable film came from Ken Tucker: Filmmaker Nicholas Roeg "doesn't seem to have approached the material with awe or trepidation," he wrote; Roeg has made a movie about a man's "disillusionment and ruin that also works as an adventure story."[23] In the last analysis, however, Roeg's cable adaptation of "Heart of Darkness" is simply not in the same league with *Apocalypse Now,* which will continue to be the yardstick by which subsequent screen versions of the novella will be judged.

Chapter 9

Epilogue:
Two Film Versions of *Nostromo*

Nostromo was filmed in the silent era, and now a remake is in preparation. Hence I have placed my brief discussion of the silent version of *Nostromo,* entitled *The Silver Treasure,* of which no known copies survive, near the end of this book, in order to link it with the remake.

Nostromo: The Novel

Conrad recalls in his "Author's Note" to *Nostromo* in the Collected Edition that around 1875 he heard tell of the sailor who would later serve as the model for the central character in *Nostromo.* The sailor in question was supposed to have stolen singlehandedly a whole lighter of silver which he claimed had sunk to the bottom of the sea when it was being transferred to the secret island where its rightful owners wished to store it. By selling bars of silver from this precious horde on the black market from time to time, the sailor was able slowly to enrich himself.

Conrad forgot about this incident for a couple of decades until he came across a volume he picked up in a secondhand bookstore. It was entitled *On Many Seas: The Life and Exploits of a Yankee Sailor.* It was written by Frederick Benton Williams (pseudonym of Herbert Elliot Hamblin) and edited by William Stone Beach. In the book the sailor is known as Nicolo. "In the sailor's story, Conrad writes in his "Note," he is presented as "an unmitigated rascal, a small cheat, stupidly ferocious, morose, and of mean appearance." Conrad thought it interesting that Nicolo would boast of his theft openly. "People think I make a lot of money in this schooner of mine; but it is nothing," Nicolo would say. His real source of income, Nicolo added, was from the sale of the bars of silver he had buried on an island near the port where he lived.

Once, in a quarrel with another sailor, the latter threatened that he would report Nicolo to the authorities for having stolen this rich supply of silver from its rightful owners. The ruffian replied that no one could prove that the treasure had not sunk in the open sea, just as he had claimed that it had. In addition, Nicolo concluded, "I didn't show you where the silver is hidden, did I? So you know nothing."

Initially, Conrad saw nothing in this anecdote that could serve as a basis of a novel. It was only when it dawned on him that, as he put it, "the purloiner of the treasure need not necessarily be a confirmed rogue, that he could even be a man of character," that Conrad began to envision the story of Nostromo (which is what he named the character in the novel), an Italian sailor living in South America who becomes rich by commandeering a horde of silver for his private use.[1] By making Nostromo a man of principle, Conrad was able to portray the crisis of conscience that someone who had been honest all his life experiences when he succumbs to the temptation of greed.

To flesh out the character of Nostromo as he appears in the novel, Conrad modeled his hero on a sailor named Dominic Cervoni, whom he had known as a youngster when he was serving as a steward on a French vessel in 1876. In his autobiographical book, *The Mirror of the Sea,* Conrad writes of Cervoni, "There was nothing in the world sudden enough to take Dominic unawares. His thick black moustaches, curled every morning with hot tongs by a barber, . . . seemed to hide a perpetual smile." Conrad goes on to say that in Dominic's eyes there lurked a look of irony, "as though he had been provided with an extremely experienced soul, and the slightest distention of his nostrils would give to his bronzed face a look of extraordinary boldness."[2]

Jeremy Hawthorne observes that "the word 'adventurer' is an important one for Conrad; and his use of it demonstrates quite clearly his awareness of the fact that Europeans who claimed that they were seeking adventure" by seeking their fortunes in

the third world "might actually be better described as adventur-
ers—individuals seeking plunder." Certainly Nostromo, as portrayed by Conrad in the novel, is such an adventurer. Nostromo, notes Hawthorne, "ends up despising himself and his
secret enslavement to the silver," the plunder he has stolen.[3]

As a matter of fact, a tragic fate overcomes Nostromo when
he happens to hide the silver treasure on an island which also is
the site of a lighthouse. One dark night when Nostromo goes to
the island to dig up some of his buried treasure, Georgio Viola,
the keeper of the lighthouse, mistakes Nostromo for Ramirez,
an unwelcome suitor who has come to elope with his daughter
Giselle. He shoots Nostromo dead, and only learns later of his
tragic mistake. Nostromo's life thus comes to an ignominious
end when he is engaged in the very act of stealing more silver
from his ill-gotten horde.

The Silver Treasure (1926): The Silent Film of Nostromo

In producing *Nostromo* as *The Silver Treasure* on the screen, the
studio executives feared that the mass audience might not be
attracted by a film with the novel's tragic ending. Accordingly,
they insisted that the film have a happy ending, whereby Nostromo suffers an attack of conscience after appropriating the
silver for himself. Consequently in the film Nostromo, who is
played by George O'Brien *(Sunrise),* acknowledges his guilt to
the owner of the mine from which he stole the silver, and
returns it to its rightful owner. The mine owner then compli-
ments Nostromo for his change of heart, and the movie ends
on this happy note.

"At the level of his mature creative insight," Hawthorne
opines, "Conrad saw clearly that there were two sides to the
term 'adventurer.' There was the glamorous side—the romantic
life pictured in adventure stories for boys. And there was the
dark underside of . . . plunder."[4] In retooling Conrad's tragic
hero in *The Silver Treasure* into a conventional movie hero,
then, the filmmakers suppressed "the dark underside" of Conrad's adventurer, and emphasized his "glamorous side." In so
doing, the filmmakers turned Conrad's dark tale of greed into
what Hawthorne terms a boy's adventure story. By all accounts

The Silver Treasure was a serviceable adventure picture with a good performance by matinee idol George O'Brien, who played the romantic hero to the hilt.

A Remake of Nostromo

Even as we come to the end of this study of the movies based on Conrad's fiction, a remake of *Nostromo* is being prepared. Initially British director David Lean *(Lawrence of Arabia)* had planned a remake of *Nostromo*. As it happened, it was scriptwriter Robert Bolt *(Lawrence of Arabia)* who first interested Lean in the novel; and together they collaborated on a screenplay, along with British playwright Christopher Hampton.[5] But the project was aborted for the time being when Lean died in April, 1991. Serge Silberman, Lean's producer, in due course interested British director Hugh Hudson *(Chariots of Fire)* in the project, and so the production is once more on the rails.

Lean had originally contacted Christopher Hampton in 1986 to collaborate with him on a script for *Nostromo*. After a year of laboring with Lean on no less than six drafts of the screenplay, Hampton left the project to move on to writing his Oscar-winning screenplay for *Dangerous Liaisons,* based on his own play. Lean then turned to Robert Bolt to carry on the work of adapting *Nostromo* for film.

When Silberman resuscitated the project a couple of years after Lean's death, he re-enlisted Hampton to provide the final screenplay for the movie. Hampton subsequently composed a version of the script which was totally his own, and did not draw on the version Robert Bolt worked on after he had left the project. The central image of both Hampton's final screenplay and of Conrad's novel is the silver of the South American silver mine about which the plot turns. As we know from the first screen adaptation of *Nostromo,* Nostromo, the hero, steals silver from the mine in order to enrich himself. The silver thus symbolizes human greed throughout the script, as it does in the novel. As Hampton has noted, his screenplay dwells to a considerable degree on the silver. Hudson and Silberman hope to shoot the film in the Pacific Northwest and Mexico. That the movie will be a faithful rendition of the novel is augured by the fact that Hampton has stayed close to his literary source in creating his screen adaptation of the novel. So Conrad's association with the cinema is by no means at an end.

Chapter 10

Conclusion: From Page to Screen

My task which I am trying to achieve is, by the power of the written word, to make you hear, to make you feel—it is, before all, to make you *see.*

—Joseph Conrad

I believe that [all of Conrad's stories] will one day be shown on the screen.

—Jessie Conrad

Giddings, Selby, and Wensley state in *Screening the Novel*, "It has become traditional in books concerned with screening the novel to open with the statements by Joseph Conrad, the novelist, and D. W. Griffith, the filmmaker, which seem almost to echo one another."[1] To be precise, in his famous Preface to his 1897 novella *The Nigger of the Narcissus* Conrad stated, as indicated in the first epigraph to this chapter, that his task as a novelist as he saw it was, above all, "to make you see."[2] Sixteen years later, in 1913, the pioneer director D. W. Griffith said, "The task I'm trying to achieve is to make you see."[3] At first glance, it seems that both artists were saying virtually the same thing. Yet the written image, i.e., a metaphor on the printed page which the reader "sees" with the eye of the imagination, is not the same thing as the visual image which the filmgoer sees on the movie screen. In sum, the different methods of seeing, to which Conrad and Griffith are referring, are a vivid reminder that fiction belongs to the print medium while motion pictures are essentially a visual medium.

Because fiction and film are two fundamentally different artistic media, literal fidelity to a literary source is rarely if ever possible when a fictional work is adapted to the screen; and it can hardly be the criterion by which a film adaptation is judged.

Thus, in considering the adaptation of fiction to film, one must accept the inescapable fact that, as we have observed in the course of this book, expansion or compression is inevitably necessary in order to accommodate a short story or novel to the very different format of a primarily visual medium. As film scholar Maurice Yacowar has noted, the faithful adaptation "is not one that makes no changes, but one in which the changes serve the intention and thrust of the original."[4]

It cannot be too often emphasized that the faithful film adaptation must preserve the spirit and theme of the original work, regardless of the superficial liberties taken with the plot and dialogue of the parent work in retooling it for the screen. Giddings, Selby, and Wensley comment that, even though film was quick to establish its own "basic techniques and forms," each new film "begins afresh in its endeavor to tell in new terms *what the writer intended to say.*"[5] (Emphasis added.) In point of fact, Conrad's thematic vision, as found in his fiction, is implicitly present in varying degrees in most of the motion pictures based on his work.

Although Conrad made no attempt to expound a coherent philosophy in his fiction, his personal vision, as noted above, was a deeply religious one. Again and again Conrad implies in his fiction that one gains salvation through sacrifice and suffering; and the concept of redemption through sacrificial suffering is, as he himself suggested, one of the central tenets of the Christian faith.

In examining the screen adaptations of Conrad's fiction discussed in this book, one finds that the impact of this same theme of redemptive suffering resonates in many of his films as well. To give two obvious examples: The heroine of *Laughing Anne* redeems her wayward life by saving Davidson's life at the expense of losing her own. Moreover, *The Rover* remains faithful to Conrad's thematic vision in portraying the manner in which Peyrol redeems the transgressions of a lifetime by sacrificing his life for the French war effort.

The majority of the screen versions of Conrad's work retain enough of the spirit of the author's originals to be regarded as fundamentally faithful to their respective literary sources. All of the Conrad films, regardless of their individual shortcomings, invariably contain at least a few moments which do Conrad justice; such scenes have been cited throughout this book.

One problem that certainly militated against the creation of authentic versions of Conrad's fiction, however, was the commercial considerations that dictated arbitrary changes calculated to bring the film versions more into line with what producers thought to be the expectations and preferences of the mass audience. Thus happy endings were manufactured for several of the early Conrad films, simply because the studios assumed that most moviegoers would stay away from a motion picture that ended unhappily as many of Conrad's stories do. "Apropos of endings," Rick Altman notes in a 1992 essay, "David Bordwell points out that 'of one hundred randomly sampled Hollywood films, over sixty ended with a display of the united romantic couple—the cliché ending, often with a clinch—and many more could be said to end happily.'"[6]

There is no doubt this concession to popular taste caused alterations in the film adaptations of Conrad's works, and that they to some degree distorted the spirit and thematic meaning of these same works.

For example, a happy ending was imposed on all three of the cinematic versions of *Victory* that we have considered, as we have seen. Indeed, at the conclusion of the second version of the novel, *Dangerous Paradise,* the villain, who is irredeemably perverse in Conrad's novel, and the hero are finally reconciled and wind up parting friends! In brief, the three films derived from *Victory* were not faithful to the essential spirit of the source story from which they were drawn.

Film scholar Regina Fadiman contends that fidelity to the original work on which a film is based is not necessarily an appropriate norm by which to evaluate the movie in question. A motion picture, she insists, must ultimately be judged on its own merits. It is true that the relationship of a film to the work of literature on which it is based is not the sole criterion by which a movie can be appraised; one can use other criteria as well, such as its place in the total canon of the movies made by the director—especially if he is an eminent film maker like Carol Reed or Richard Brooks. Nonetheless, studying a film in terms of the fictional work which inspired it remains a fruitful critical pursuit.

To take one example, one cannot adequately comprehend the way in which elements of Conrad's *Heart of Darkness,* such as the journey upriver in search of Kurtz, were effectively integrated into *Apocalypse Now,* which updated the story to the Vietnam War, unless one carefully examines the novella on which the movie was based. Furthermore, there is little doubt that films based on the work of a major novelist such as Conrad gain interest precisely because they are associated with the canon of a great writer. And even when a particular movie fails to do justice to its literary source, it can sometimes tell us as much about the relationship of the two media as one that is artistically more successful.

Film makers continue to look to Conrad's fiction as a source for films. Andrew Gillon wrote an interesting article in *Conradiana* about his efforts to mount a production of his film adaptation of *Under Western Eyes,* which novel, of course, had been filmed in France as *Razumov.* Gillon, who worked on the script with the assistance of Polish film maker Witold Orzehowski, received a grant from the National Endowment for the Humanities to develop a screenplay for the film. Gillon subsequently submitted their labors to the Endowment, but unfortunately further funding for a production grant was not forthcoming from NEH.

The NEH panelists, who examined no less than three different versions of the screenplay, dubbed Gillon's final effort as "uneven," and concluded their observations as follows: "Though exhibiting a sensitivity and fidelity to the novel at many points, [the script] has serious weaknesses; and hence the Endowment cannot offer a production grant." Gillon's final reflection on his ordeal is simply, "The life of a screenwriter aspiring to adapt this Conrad novel is not an easy one."[7]

Fiction versus Television

One hopes that Conrad will continue to challenge those who would adapt his works to the visual media. It might seem at first that the television mini-series format might be better suited than the theatrical feature for presenting a screen adaptation of a Conrad novel. After all, a mini-series has more screen time to devote to the plot of one of Conrad's long novels like *Lord Jim* than does a feature length film. "A television adaptation of a novel will often devote several hours to its material, often in weekly serial form," Giddings, Selby, and Wensley write.[8] Morris Beja adds, "When a three-hundred-page novel is made into a two-or three-hour movie, a great deal will have to be sacrificed. Less will be lost in a television serial, to be sure, which may last from eight to ten or even twelve hours."[9]

But not even a mini-series can capture the full scope of a novel like *Lord Jim*. TV producer Stan Margulies *(The Thorn Birds)* admits frankly that one of the problems inherent in working in television is that "you are locked into an inexorable time frame." If any of the installments of a mini-series exceeds the stipulated running time determined in advance by network executives, it will simply have to be shortened to the required running time. "The scenes that have to come out are inevitably the scenes devoted to character rather than plot," explains Margulies; "and I hate to lose those scenes."

Furthermore, feature motion pictures are made with more polish and care than telefilms of whatever length. The makers of a theatrical feature have the luxury of reshooting a scene until it is satisfactory; that is not the case with a television movie. Richard Chamberlain *(The Thorn Birds)* concedes that "you want to do things over again, and you don't have the time."[10] One recalls in this context TV journalist Kathleen Fury's observation that telefilms, in contrast to theatrical films, are made on the double and on the cheap. Consequently, a finely crafted theatrical feature drawn from a novel will not automatically be overshadowed by a television mini-series derived from the same work.

For example, a three-part television adaptation of *The Secret Agent* was aired on PBS in late 1992. Hitchcock, of course, had filmed Conrad's novel in 1936 as *Sabotage*. Almost invariably when a Hitchcock movie has been remade by other hands, the remake, while perhaps alright when considered by itself, suffers by comparison with the original, in much the same manner that the road company version of a Broadway play is so often judged inferior to the original production. The TV version of *The Secret Agent* is surely no exception to this rule. The listless telefilm simply lacks the panache and flair that Hitchcock invested in *Sabotage*. Whenever he was asked what he thought of the remake of one of his movies, Hitchcock would always respond laconically, "What remake? I only know one." To a large extent there *is* only one true version of any film he made. His. [11] (By the same token, there is no way that the 1994 cable TV film of *Heart of Darkness* could approximate the depth and scope of *Apocalypse Now.*)

In summary, a carefully made feature film version of novel, such as Hitchcock's adaptation of *The Secret Agent,* is not automatically overshadowed by the TV mini-series made from the same work, for the reasons advanced by one of TV's own top producers and stars. In addition, whether or not Conrad's fiction should be turned into television mini-series may be a moot point, since the mini-series format has become prohibitively expensive, to the extent that one TV commentator in *The New York Times* recently opined that in the not-too-distant future the TV mini-series may well be a thing of the past.

Perhaps television is best suited to dramatizing short fiction which can be presented comfortably in a one-hour time frame. In this context one recalls the two excellent film adaptations of Conrad's "Secret Sharer": although they were not made for TV, they both had a running time of less than an hour. This approach to adapting short fiction to a visual medium, as said before, eliminates the need to extend the plotline of the original short story to the degree that is called for by making it into a feature-length film, as happened in the case of *Laughing Anne.*

L'Envoi

Conrad's achievement as a major English novelist is generally recognized. But to what extent, in the last analysis, was the impact of his fiction transferred to the films that were adapted from it? In looking back on the Conrad motion pictures discussed in this book, one must concede that none of them is pure Conrad; and even the best of them is not flawless. As a matter of fact, some Conrad commentators claim that his subtle, evocative prose simply resists being transferred successfully to another medium of artistic expression. Nevertheless, many of the films of Conrad's fiction have proved to be rewarding cinematic experiences, and some represent excellent examples of the art of adapting a fictional work to the screen.

Preserving the spirit of Conrad's fictional works on film with taste and discrimination calls for gifted screenwriters and directors; and the Conrad films have attracted some of the best, as we have had occasion to note in the course of this book: from scriptwriters like Jules Furthman and John Milius to directors like Alfred Hitchcock and Francis Coppola. In addition, some actors have done some of the best work of their careers in Conrad-based films; and this is particularly true of Peter O'Toole's performance in the 1965 *Lord Jim*. Another case in point is Martin Sheen, whose work in *Apocalypse Now* marked the peak of his career as an actor. Moreover, the best of these films—*An Outcast of the Islands, The Duellists,* and *Apocalypse Now*—deserve to rank as screen classics, while four others—both versions of *Lord Jim, Razumov,* and *Sabotage*—are not far behind.

The great American crime writer James M. Cain *(Double Indemnity)* once remarked that he had rarely gone to see the screen version of one of his novels. "People tell me, don't you *care* what they've done to your book? I tell them, they haven't done anything to my book. It's right there on the shelf. They paid me and that's the end of it."[12] John Updike writes in a similar vein that the text of a novel that has been filmed remains available for the reader to stumble upon: "The text is almost infinitely patient, snugly gathering its dust on the shelf; . . . the text remains readily recoverable and potentially as alive as the day it was scribbled," while the movie version of it may have long since been forgotten.[13] What both novelists are saying is that movies come and go, while the books from which they were derived have the longer life.

On the contrary, in Conrad's case, a number of the films drawn from his work remain accessible for viewing as reruns on television, and through the 16mm and videocassette channels of distribution. They continue to be seen, just as the books continue to be read. Furthermore, I think it is a safe bet that the best of the Conrad films, with *Apocalypse Now* leading the list, will last as long as anything he has written. Indeed, the best of these films are an enduring tribute to his achievement as a writer.

Notes

Introduction

1. Joy Gould Boyum, *Double Exposure: Fiction into Film* (New York: New American Library, 1985), p. 4; p. 6.

2. Alfred Hitchcock, "Film Production," *Encyclopedia Britannica*, vol. 15 (1972), 908.

3. Rick Altman, "Dickens, Griffith, and Film Theory Today," in *Classical Hollywood Narrative*, ed. Jane Gaines (Durham: Duke University Press, 1992), p. 11; p. 18.

4. Robert Nathan, "A Novelist Looks at Hollywood," in *Film: A Montage of Theories*, ed. Richard Dyer McCann (New York: Dutton, 1966), p. 130.

5. Quoted by A. R. Fulton, *Motion Pictures: The Development of an Art* (Norman: University of Oklahoma Press, 1970), p. 125.

6. Jerry Wald, "Screen Adaptation," *Films in Review* 5 (February, 1954), 65-66.

7. A. E. Hotchner, "One Thing after Another: The Adaptation," in *The Eighth Art: Twenty-Three Views of TV Today* (New York: Holt, Rinehart, and Winston, 1962), p. 72; p. 76.

8. Quoted by Richard Corliss, *Talking Pictures: Screenwriters in the American Cinema* (New York: Penguin, 1975), p. 263.

9. Robert Gidding, Keith Selby, and Chris Wensley, *Screening the Novel: The Theory and Practice of Literary Adaptation* (New York: St. Martin's Press, 1990), p. 9. The three authors do not distinguish who wrote which portions of the text; hence I must mention all three names when citing this work.

10. George Bluestone, *Novels into Film* (Berkeley: University of California Press, 1961), pp. 62-63.

11. Charles Barr, "Cinemascope: Before and After," in *Film: A Montage of Theories*, ed. Richard Dyer McCann, p. 323.

12. Giddings, Selby, and Wensley, *Screening the Novel*, p. xiv.

13. Regina K. Fadiman, *Faulkner's Intruder in the Dust: Novel into Film* (Knoxville: University of Tennessee Press, 1978), p. 9.

14. Wald, "Screen Adaptation," 65.

15. Edward Murray, *The Cinematic Imagination: Writers and the Motion Picture* (New York: Ungar, 1972).

16. Avron Fleishman, *Narrated Films: Storytelling Situations in Cinema History* (Baltimore: Johns Hopkins University Press, 1992), p. 12; p. 78-79.

17. Bruce Bawer, *The Screenplay's the Thing* (Hamden, Conn.: Archon Books, 1992), p. 4.

18. Wald, "Screen Adaptations," 67.

19. John Lester, *Conrad and Religion* (New York: St. Martin's Press, 1988), p. 19.

20. John Conrad, *Joseph Conrad: Times Remembered* (New York: Cambridge University Press, 1981), p. 152.

21. John Updike, "Seen the Film? Read the Book!" *New York Times,* June 28, 1987, sec. 2:1.

22. Graham Greene, "Preface," *Three Plays* (London: Mercury Books, 1961), p. xiii; cf. Graham Greene, "The Novelist and the Cinema: A Personal Experience," in *International Film Annual,* no. 2 (New York: Doubleday, 1958), p. 58.

23. Quoted by David Lodge, "Graham Greene," *The Tablet* (London), September 28, 1974, p. 937.

24. Quoted by Morris Beja, *Film and Literature* (New York: Longman, 1979), p. 27.

25. Quoted by Sheilah Graham, *College for One* (New York: Viking, 1967), p. 167.

26. Michiko Kakutani, "Books into Movies," *New York Times Book Review,* July 10, 1083, p. 39.

27. Quoted by Gene Phillips, *Stanley Kubrick: A Film Odyssey* (New York: Popular Library, 1977), pp. 105-106.

28. Quoted by Gene Phillips, *John Schlesinger* (Boston: Twayne, 1981), p. 82; p. 90.

29. Gidding, Selby, and Wensley, *Screening the Novel,* p. xix.

30. Arthur Hoomberg, "Proust Filmed at Last," *New York Times,* January 14, 1983, sec. 2:15.

Chapter 1

1. Joseph Conrad, *A Personal Record* (New York: Doubleday, 1925), Collected Edition, p. 122.

2. Borys Conrad, *My Father: Joseph Conrad* (New York: Coward-McCann, 1970), p. 148.

3. Joseph Conrad to J. B. Pinker, June 17, 1919. Unpublished Letter, in the Berg Collection of the New York Public Library.

4. Joseph Conrad, *Letters to a Friend,* ed. Richard Curle (New York: Doubleday, Doran, 1928), p. 87; p. 90. N.B.: Conrad's scenario should not be confused with the 1926 film of the same name, starring the silent film comedian Harry Langdon.

5. Jeffrey Meyers, *Joseph Conrad: A Biography* (New York: Scribner's, 1991), p. 340.

6. Mordaunt Hall, "The Screen: *The Road to Romance,*" *New York Times,* October 10, 1927, p. 24.

7. Joseph Conrad, *The Collected Letters,* eds. Frederick Karl and Lawrence Davies (Cambridge University Press, 1983), I, 288; II, 49.

8. Heliéna Krenn, *Conrad's Lingard Trilogy: Empire, Race, and Women in the Maylay Novels* (New York: Garland, 1990), pp. 125-26.

9. *Ibid.,* p. 101.

Chapter 2

1. Joseph Conrad, "Author's Note," *Victory* (New York: Doubleday, 1925), the Collected Edition, p. xi.

2. Frederick Karl, *Joseph Conrad: The Three Lives* (New York: Farrar, Straus, and Giroux), p. 145.

3. Conrad, "Author's Note," *Victory,* p. xii; p. xv; p. xvi. (Page references to the text of the novel will appear in parentheses after each citation from it.)

4. Carl D. Bennett, *Joseph Conrad* (New York: Continuum, 1991), p. 118.

5. Frederick Karl, *A Reader's Guide to Conrad,* rev. ed. (New York: Farrar, Straus, and Giroux, 1979), p. 265.

6. Catharine Rising, *Darkness at Heart: Fathers and Sons in Conrad* (New York: Greenwood Press, 1990), p. 142.

7. *Ibid.,* p. 143.

8. *Ibid.,* p. 146.

9. Liam O'Leary, "Maurice Tourneur," in *The International Dictionary of Films and Filmmakers,* rev. ed., ed. Nicholas Thomas (London: St. James Press, 1991), vol. 2, 840.

10. *Ibid.*

11. Karl, *Joseph Conrad,* p. 849.

12. Frank Thompson, *William A. Wellman* (Metuchen, N.J.: Scarecrow Press, 1983), p. 96; p. 94.

13. Stephen Hanson, "William A. Wellman," in *The International Dictionary of Films and Filmmakers,* rev. ed., ed. Nicholas Thomas (London: St. James Press, 1991), vol. 2, 908.

14. William C. Houze, "Philosophy, Politics, and Morality in *The Secret Agent* as Novel and Play: A Comparative Study," Unpublished Ph.D. Dissertation (Syracuse, N.Y.: Syracuse University, 1980), p. 80.

15. Kingsley Canham, "John Cromwell," in *The Hollywood Professionals,* vol. 5 (New York: Barnes, 1976), 94.

16. Stephen Land, *Paradox and Polarity in the Fiction of Joseph Conrad* (New York: St. Martin's Press, 1984), p. 196.

17. Quoted by William Thomaier, "Conrad on the Screen," *Films in Review* 21, no. 2 (December, 1970), 617.

18. Canham, "Cromwell," *Hollywood Professionals,* vol. 5, 94.

Chapter 3

1. Joseph Conrad, "Author's Note," *A Personal Record* (New York: Doubleday, 1925), the Collected Edition, p. viii; p. x.

2. Joseph Conrad, "Author's Note," *Under Western Eyes* (New York: Doubleday, 1925), the Collected Edition, p. ix. (Page references to the text of the novel will appear in parentheses after each citation from it.)

3. Quoted by Jeffrey Myers, *Joseph Conrad* (New York: Scribner's, 1991), p. 252.

4. Keith Carabine, "'Figure Behind the Veil': Conrad and Razumov in *Under Western Eyes,*" in *Joseph Conrad's Under Western Eyes: Beginnings,*

Revisions, Final Forms: Five Essays, ed. David R. Smith (Hamden, Conn.: Archon Books, 1991), p. 2; p. 16.

5. Eloise Knapp Hay, "*Under Western Eyes* and the Missing Center," in *Joseph Conrad's Under Western Eyes,* ed. David R. Smith, p. 142.

6. Quoted by Myers, *Joseph Conrad,* p. 252.

7. Roderick Davis, "Crossing the Dark Roadway: Razumov on the Boulevard des Philosophes," in *Joseph Conrad's Under Western Eyes,* ed. David R. Smith, p. 161.

8. Pauline Kael, *5001 Nights at the Movies* (New York: Holt, Rinehart, and Winston, 1991), p. 617.

9. Steve Vineberg, "The Routes into Conrad on Filming: *Under Western Eyes* and *An Outcast of the Islands,*" *Literature/Film Quarterly* 15, no. 1 (Winter, 1987), 24.

10. Joseph Conrad, "Author's Note," *The Secret Agent: A Simple Tale* (New York: Doubleday, 1925), the Collected Edition, p. ix; p. x. (Page references to the text of the novel will appear in parentheses after each citation from it.)

11. Jeremy Hawthorn, *Joseph Conrad: Narrative Technique and Ideological Commitment* (London: Edward Arnold, 1990), p. 77.

12. Leo Gurko, *Joseph Conrad: Giant in Exile* (New York: Collier Books, 1979), p. 171.

13. Catharine Rising, *Darkness at Heart: Fathers and Sons in Conrad* (New York: Greenwood Press, 1990), p. 110.

14. Joseph Conrad, "Stephen Crane," in *Last Essays,* ed. Richard Curle (New York: Doubleday, 1926), p. 116.

15. Paul Kirschner, "Conrad and the Film," *Quarterly of Radio, TV, and Film* 11 (Summer, 1957), 348.

16. Roger Tennant, *Joseph Conrad* (New York: Atheneum, 1981), p. 240; cf. Joseph Conrad, *The Secret Agent: A Drama in Fours Acts* in Joseph Conrad and Ford Madox Ford, *In the Nature of a Crime, and Three Works by Joseph Conrad* (New York: Doubleday, 1926). For the record, Conrad reduced the four-act version of the play to three acts for production at the Ambassador Theater in 1922. He did so by the simple expedient of adding the original Act III onto the end of Act II (as Act II, scene iii), and thus designated the original Act IV as Act III. Conrad chose to do this presumably to shorten the running time of the play by eliminating the intermission between the original Act III and the original Act IV.

17. William C. Houze, "Philosophy, Politics, and Morality in *The Secret Agent* as Novel and Play: A Comparative Study," Unpublished Ph.D. Disserta-

tion (Syracuse, N.Y.: Syracuse University, 1980), pp. 114, 118. An abridged version of this thesis appears under the title "*The Secret Agent* from Novel to Play: The Implications of Conrad's Handling of Structure," *Conradiana* 13, no. 2 (Summer, 1981), 109-27.

18. Houze, "*The Secret Agent* as Novel and Play," p. 84.

19. John Batchelor, *The Life of Joseph Conrad: A Critical Biography* (Cambridge, Mass.: Blackwell, 1994), p. 275.

20. Frederick Karl, *Conrad: The Three Lives* (New York: Farrar, Straus, and Giroux, 1979), p. 849.

21. Earl G. Ingersoll, "Cinematic Effects in Conrad's *Secret Agent,*" *Conradiana* 21, no. 1 (Spring, 1989), 29.

22. Michael A. Anderegg, "Conrad and Hitchcock: *The Secret Agent* Inspires *Sabotage,*" *Literature/Film Quarterly* 3 (Summer, 1973), 224.

23. Donald Spoto, *The Art of Alfred Hitchcock,* 2nd ed. (New York: Anchor Books, 1992), pp. 58-59.

24. Anderegg, "Conrad and Hitchcock," p. 218.

25. *Ibid.,* p. 223.

26. Alfred Hitchcock, "Direction," in Albert J. LaValley, ed. *Focus on Hitchcock* (Englewood Cliffs, N.J.: Prentice-Hall, 1972), pp. 34-35.

27. Cf. Paula M. Cohen, "*The Secret Agent* and *Sabotage.*" *Literature/Film Quarterly* 22, no. 3 (1994), 207.

28. Hitchcock, "Direction," p. 34.

Chapter 4

1. Joseph Conrad, "Author's Note," *An Outcast of the Islands* (New York: Doubleday, 1925), the Collected Edition, p. ix; p. x. (Page references to the text of the novel will appear in parentheses after each citation from it.)

2. Joseph Conrad, *A Personal Record* (New York: Doubleday, 1925), the Collected Edition, pp. 74-75.

3. Heliéna Krenn, *Conrad's Lingard Trilogy: Empire, Race, and Women in the Maylay Novels* (New York: Garland, 1990), p. 57.

4. Ruth Nadelhaft, *Joseph Conrad* (Atlantic Highlands, N.J.: Humanities Press International, 1991), p. 30.

5. Stephen Land, *Paradox and Polarity in the Fiction of Joseph Conrad* (New York: St. Martin's Press, 1984), p. 32.

6. Krenn, *Conrad's Lingard Trilogy*, p. 57.

7. Land, *Paradox and Polarity in the Fiction of Joseph Conrad*, p. 32.

8. Krenn, *Conrad's Lingard Trilogy*, p. 62.

9. Charles Thomas Samuels, "Sir Carol Reed," *Encountering Directors* (New York: Capricorn, 1972), p. 166.

10. Jerome Moss, *The Films of Carol Reed* (New York: Columbia University Press, 1987), p. 198.

11. *Ibid.*, p. 203.

12. Marcia Landy, *British Genres: Cinema and Society, 1930-60* (Princeton, N.J.: Princeton University Press, 1991), p. 33.

13. Wallace Watson, "Conrad and Film," *Conradiana* 11, no. 3 (1979), 223.

14. Gene D. Phillips, *Major Film Directors of the American and British Cinema* (Cranbury, N.J.: Associated University Presses, 1990), p. 174.

15. Watson, "Conrad and Cinema," 224.

16. See Nicholas Wapshott, *Carol Reed: A Biography* (New York: Knopf, 1994), pp. 229-44, on this film.

17. Samuels, "Carol Reed," p. 166.

18. Brian McFarland, ed., *Sixty Voices: Celebrities Recall the Golden Age of British Cinema* (London: British Film Institute, 1992), p. 123.

19. Pauline Kael, *Kiss Kiss Bang Bang* (New York: Bantam Books, 1969), p. 410.

20. Moss, *Carol Reed*, p. 197.

Chapter 5

1. Carl D. Bennett, *Joseph Conrad* (New York: Continuum, 1991), p. 113.

2. Joseph Conrad, "The Secret Sharer," in *The Shorter Tales of Joseph Conrad* (New York: Doubleday, 1924), pp. 44-46. (Subsequent page references to the text of the story will appear after each citation from it.)

3. Frederick Karl, *A Reader's Guide to Joseph Conrad*, rev. ed. (New York: Farrar, Straus, and Giroux, 1970), p. 234.

4. Bennett, *Joseph Conrad*, p. 113; p. 114.

5. Conrad, "Preface," *The Shorter Tales*, p. xi.

6. Catharine Rising, *Darkness at Heart: Fathers and Sons in Conrad* (New York: Greenwood Press, 1990), p. 118.

7. *Ibid.*

8. Quoted by Geoffrey Wagner, *The Novel and the Cinema* (Cranbury, N.J.: Associated University Presses, 1975), p. 207.

9. Leo Gurko, *Joseph Conrad: Giant in Exile* (New York: Collier Books, 1979), p. 222.

10. John Galsworthy, "Introduction," *Laughing Anne, and One Day More: Two Plays by Joseph Conrad* (London: John Castle, 1924), p. ix.

11. John Batchelor, *The Life of Joseph Conrad* (Cambridge, Mass.: Blackwell, 1994), pp. 22-23.

12. Avrom Fleishman, *Narrated Films: Storytelling Situations in Cinema History* (Baltimore: Johns Hopkins University Press, 1992), p. 78.

13. Joseph Conrad, "Because of the Dollars," in *The Shorter Tales*, p. 287.

14. Jerry Vermilye, "Margaret Lockwood: Part II," *Films in Review* 42, nos. 3/4 (March/April, 1991), 88.

Chapter 6

1. Joseph Conrad, "Author's Note," *Lord Jim: A Tale* (New York: Doubleday, 1925), the Collected Edition, p. ix. (Page references to the text of the novel will appear in parentheses after each citation from it.)

2. Ross Murfin, *Lord Jim: After the Truth* (New York: Twayne, 1991), p. 46.

3. *Ibid.*, p. 57.

4. Leo Gurko, *Joseph Conrad: Giant in Exile* (New York: Collier Books, 1979), pp. 107-108.

5. *Ibid.*, p. 107.

6. Murfin, *Lord Jim: After the Truth*, p. 74.

7. *Ibid.*, p. 107.

8. Gurko, *Joseph Conrad*, pp. 108-109.

9. Murfin, *Lord Jim: After the Truth*, p. 114.

10. Jeanine Basinger, "Victor Fleming," in *The International Dictionary of Films and Filmmakers*, rev. ed., ed. Nicholas Thomas (London: St. James Press, 1991), vol. 2., 289.

11. Mordaunt Hall, "The Screen: *Lord Jim,*" *New York Times,* November 6, 1924, n.p.

12. Graham Greene, *Graham Greene on Film* (New York: Simon and Schuster, 1972), p. 162.

13. Hall, *"Lord Jim,"* n.p.

14. "Best of the New Films," *Catholic Film Newsletter* 30, no. 5 (April, 1965), 3.

15. Frank Frost, "The Films of Richard Brooks," Unpublished Ph.D. Dissertation (Los Angeles: University of Southern California, 1976), p. 234; cf. Patrick McGilligan, "Interview with Richard Brooks," in *Backstory 2: Interviews with Screenwriters,* ed. Patrick McGilligan (Berkeley: University of California Press, 1991), pp. 60, ff.

16. Bernard Kantor, Irwin R. Blacker, and Anne Kramer, eds. *Directors at Work: Interviews with American Film Makers* (New York: Funk and Wagnalls, 1970), p. 11.

17. *Ibid.,* p. 12.

18. Adam Gillon, *Joseph Conrad* (Boston: Twayne, 1982), p. 185.

19. Hollis Alpert, "A Director Redeems Himself," *Saturday Review,* March 6, 1965, p. 39.

20. Frost, "The Films of Richard Brooks," p. 236.

21. V. F. Perkins, *Film as Film* (New York: Penguin, 1978), pp. 82-83.

22. Alpert, "A Director Redeems Himself," p. 39.

23. John Baxter, "Richard Brooks," in *The International Dictionary of Films and Filmmakers,* vol. 2, 103.

24. Alpert, "A Director Redeems Himself," p. 39.

Chapter 7

1. Catharine Rising, *Darkness at Heart: Fathers and Sons in Conrad* (New York: Greenwood Press, 1990), p. 160.

2. Joseph Conrad, *The Rover* (New York: Doubleday, 1925), the Collected Edition, p. 174; p. 267.

3. Rising, *Darkness at Heart,* p. 159; p. 156.

4. Quoted by Gene Ringgold, *The Films of Rita Hayworth* (Secaucus, N.J.: Citadel Press, 1974), p. 239.

5. Joseph Conrad, "Author's Note," *A Set of Six* (New York: Doubleday, 1925), the Collected Edition, p. ix. (Page references to the text of the story will appear in parentheses after each citation from it.)

6. Ruth Nadelhaft, *Joseph Conrad* (Atlantic Highlands, N.J.: Humanities Press International, 1991), p. 67.

7. Quoted by Adam Gillon, *Joseph Conrad* (Boston: Twayne, 1982), p. 137.

8. Susan Doll, "Ridley Scott," in *The International Dictionary of Films and Filmmakers,* rev. ed., ed. Nicholas Thomas (London: St. James Press, 1991), vol. 2, 761.

9. Quoted by Janet McLauchlan, "'The Duel' and *The Duellists,*" *Joseph Conrad Today* 4, no. 4 (July, 1979), 121.

10. Pauline Kael, *When the Lights Go Down* (New York: Holt, Rinehart, and Winston, 1980), p. 383.

11. Roderick Davis, "New Adaptation of Conrad," *Joseph Conrad Today* 3, no. 4 (July, 1978), 91.

12. William Costanzo, "*The Duellists:* Transposing Conrad's Fiction to Film," *Joseph Conrad Today* 4, no. 3 (April, 1979), 117.

13. Juliet McLauchlan, "'The Duel' and *The Duellists,*" 121.

14. Roderick Davis, "Conrad Cinematized: *The Duellists,*" *Literature/Film Quarterly* 8 (Spring, 1980), 130.

Chapter 8

1. Joseph Conrad, *A Personal Record* (New York: Doubleday, 1925), the Collected Edition, p. 13.

2. Joseph Conrad, "Heart of Darkness," in *Youth and Two Other Stories* (New York: Doubleday, 1925), the Collected Edition, p. 113. (Subsequent page references to the text of the novella will appear in parentheses after each citation from it.)

3. Carl D. Bennett, *Joseph Conrad* (New York: Continuum, 1991), p. 81.

4. Adam Gillon, *Joseph Conrad* (Boston: Twayne, 1982), p. 71.

5. Catharine Rising, *Darkness at Heart: Father and Sons in Conrad* (New York: Greenwood Press, 1990), p. 49.

6. Richard Ambrosini, *Conrad's Fiction as Critical Discourse* (Cambridge: Cambridge University Press, 1991), p. 91.

7. Gillon, *Joseph Conrad,* p. 73.

8. Robert L. Carringer, *The Making of Citizen Kane* (Berkeley: University of California Press, 1985), p. 3; p. 5.

9. Jose Luis Guarner, *"The Heart of the Forest,"* *The Film Center Gazette* (Chicago) 18, no. 5 (May, 1988), 8.

10. Lawrence Suid, "Hollywood and Vietnam," *Film Comment* 15, no. 1 (September-October, 1979), 21.

11. Brooks Riley, "'Heart' Transplant," *Film Comment* 15, no. 1 (September-October, 1979), 26. Cf. Richard Thompson, "John Milius Interviewed," *Film Comment* 12, no. 4 (July-August, 1976) 10-11, which contains two script extracts from Milius's first draft of the screenplay.

12. Riley, "'Heart' Transplant," 26.

13. Tony Chui, "Francis Ford Coppola's Cinematic *Apocalypse* is Finally at Hand," *New York Times*, August 12, 1979, sec. 2:17.

14. William M. Hagen, "'Heart of Darkness' and the Process of *Apocalypse Now*," *Conradiana* 12, no. 1 (1981), 49.

15. Peter Cowie, *Coppola: The Director as Visionary* (New York: Da Capo, 1994), p. 120.

16. Linda Costanzo Cahir, "Narratological Parallels in Joseph Conrad's 'Heart of Darkness' and Francis Ford Coppola's *Apocalypse Now*," *Literature/Film Quarterly* 20, no. 3 (1992), 182-83.

17. Quoted by Gene D. Phillips, *Graham Greene: The Films of His Fiction* (New York: Columbia University Teachers College Press, 1974), p. 175.

18. Cahir, "Narratological Parallels in 'Heart of Darkness' and *Apocalypse Now*," 184.

19. Louis K. Greiff, "Soldier, Sailor, Surfer, Chef: Conrad's Ethics and the Margins of *Apocalypse Now*," *Literature/Film Quarterly* 20, no. 3 (1992), 192.

20. Joy Gould Boyum, *Double Exposure: Fiction into Film* (New York: New American Library, 1985), p. 111.

21. Quoted by Jean-Paul Chaillet and Elizabeth Vincent, *Francis Ford Coppola*, trans. Denise Raab Jacobs (New York: St. Martin's Press, 1984), p. 65.

22. Caroline Kirk Cordero, "Mistah Kurtz–He Alive," *Premiere*, March, 1994, p. 97.

23. Ken Tucker, *"Heart of Darkness* on Cable," *Entertainment Weekly*, March 11, 1994, p. 40.

Chapter 9

1. Joseph Conrad, "Author's Note," *Nostromo* (New York: Doubleday, 1925), the Collected Edition, p. viii; p. ix.

2. Joseph Conrad, *The Mirror to the Sea* (New York: Doubleday, 1925), the Collected Edition, pp. 162-63.

3. Jeremy Hawtorn, *Joseph Conrad: Narrative Techniques and Ideological Commitment* (London: Edward Arnold, 1990), p. 206.

4. *Ibid.,* p. 208.

5. Harlan Kennedy, *"Nostromo,"* *American Film* 15, no. 6 (March 1990), 27-31, 53-55.

Chapter 10

1. Robert Giddings, Keith Selby, and Chris Wensley, *Screening the Novel: The Theory and Practice of Literary Adaptation* (New York: St. Martin's Press, 1990), p. 7.

2. Joseph Conad, "Preface," *The Nigger of the Narcissus* (New York: Doubleday, 1925), the Collected Edition, p. xiv.

3. Giddings, Selby, and Wensley, *Screening the Novel,* p. 1.

4. Maurice Yacowar, *Tennessee Williams and Film* (New York: Ungar, 1977), p. 7.

5. Giddings, Selby, and Wensley, *Screening the Novel,* p. x.

6. Rick Altman, "Dickens, Griffith, and Film Theory Today," in *Classical Hollywood Narrative,* ed. Jane Gaines (Durham: Duke University Press, 1992), p. 32.

7. Adam Gillon, "Adapting Conrad to Film," *The Conradian* 13, no. 2 (December, 1988), 166, 169. This essay appears in a different form in Andrew Gillon, *Joseph Conrad: Comparative Essays,* ed. Raymond Breback (Lubbock Texas: Texas Tech University Press, 1994).

8. Giddings, Selby, and Wensley, *Screening the Novel,* p. 4.

9. Morris Beja, *Film and Literature* (New York: Longman, 1979), p. 84.

10. Stephen Farber, "Making Book on TV," *Film Comment,* 18 no. 6 (November-December, 1986), 45; 47.

11. Quoted by Gene Phillips, *Alfred Hitchcock* (Boston: Twayne, 1984), p. 38.

12. Quoted by Gene Phillips, *Graham Greene: The Films of His Fiction* (New York: Columbia University Teachers College Press, 1974), p. 14.

13. John Updike, "Seen the Film? Read the Book!" *New York Times,* June 28, 1987, sec. 2:1, 28.

Bibliography

I. Primary Sources

(Note: The original date of publication appears after a title when the edition consulted was of a later date.)

Joseph Conrad. *The Collected Letters*. Edited by Frederick Karl and Lawrence Davies. I.: 1861-97; II: 1898-1902; III: 1903-1907; IV: 1908-11. New York: Cambridge University Press, 1983-91.

——. *Last Essays*. Edited by Richard Curle. New York: Doubleday, 1926.

——. *Laughing Anne, and One Day More: Two Plays by Joseph Conrad*. With an Introduction by John Galsworthy. London: John Castle, 1924.

——. *Letters to a Friend*. Edited by Richard Curle. New York: Doubleday, Doran, 1928.

——. *Letters to Edward Garnett*. Edited by Edward Garnett. Indianapolis: Bobbs-Merrill, 1928.

——. *Letters to R. B. Cunningham Graham*. Edited by C. T. Watts. Cambridge: Cambridge University Press, 1969.

——. *On Fiction*. Edited by Walter F. Wright. Lincoln: University of Nebraska Press, 1964.

——. *Lord Jim: A Tale* (1900). New York: Doubleday, 1925. The Collected Edition.

——. *The Mirror to the Sea,* and *A Personal Record* (1912). New York: Doubleday, 1925. The Collected Edition.

———. *The Nigger of the Narcissus* (1897). New York: Doubleday, 1925. The Collected Edition.

———. *Nostromo* (1904). New York: Doubleday, 1925. The Collected Edition.

———. *Notes on Life and Letters* (1921). New York: Doubleday, 1925. The Collected Edition.

———. *An Outcast of the Islands* (1896). New York: Doubleday, 1925. The Collected Edition.

———. *A Personal Record* (1912). New York: Doubleday, 1925. The Collected Edition.

———. *The Rescue* (1920). New York: Doubleday, 1925. The Collected Edition.

———. *Romance* (1903). New York: Doubleday, 1925. The Collected Edition.

———. *The Rover* (1923). New York: Doubleday, 1925. The Collected Edition.

———. *The Secret Agent: A Drama in Four Acts* (1921). In Joseph Conrad and Ford Madox Ford, *In the Nature of a Crime, and Three Works by Joseph Conrad*. Garden City, N.Y.: Doubleday Page, 1926.

———. *The Secret Agent: A Simple Tale* (1907). New York: Doubleday, 1925. The Collected Edition.

———. *A Set of Six* (1908). New York: Doubleday, 1925. The Collected Edition.

———. *The Shorter Tales of Joseph Conrad*. New York: Doubleday, 1924.

———. *Under Western Eyes* (1911). New York: Doubleday, 1925. The Collected Edition.

———. *Victory* (1915). New York: Doubleday, 1925. The Collected Edition.

———. *Youth and Two Other Stories* (1902). New York: Doubleday, 1925. The Collected Edition. (Includes "Heart of Darkness.")

II. Secondary Sources

(Note: Only the more significant research materials are included here; other books and articles alluded to in the text are not listed.)

A. Books

Ambrosini, Richard. *Conrad's Fiction as Critical Discourse.* Cambridge: Cambridge University Press, 1991.

Balázs, Béla. *Theory of Film.* New York: Dover, 1970.

Batchelor, John. *The Life of Joseph Conrad: A Critical Biography.* Cambridge, Mass.: Blackwell, 1994.

Bawer, Bruce. *The Screenplay's the Thing.* Hamden, Conn.: Archon Books, 1992.

Beja, Morris. *Film and Literature.* New York: Longman, 1979.

Bennett, Carl D. *Joseph Conrad.* New York: Continuum, 1991.

Billy, Ted., ed. *Critical Essays on Joseph Conrad.* Boston: Twayne, 1987.

Bluestone, George. *Novels into Film.* Berkeley: University of California Press, 1961.

Boyum, Joy Gould. *Double Exposure: Fiction into Film.* New York: New American Library, 1985.

Braudy, Leo. *Native Informant: Essays on Film, Fiction, and Popular Culture.* New York: Oxford University Press, 1991.

Carringer, Robert L. *The Making of Citizen Kane.* Berkeley: University of California Press, 1985. (Includes a section on Welles's unproduced scenario for *Heart of Darkness.*)

Chaillet, Jean Paul and Elizabeth Vincent. *Francis Ford Coppola.* New York: St. Martin's Press, 1984.

Chown, Jeffrey. *Hollywood Auteur: Francis Coppola.* New York: Praeger, 1988.

Conley, Tom. *Film Hieroglyphs: Ruptures in Classical Cinema.* Minneapolis: University of Minnesota Press, 1991.

Conrad, Borys. *My Father: Joseph Conrad.* New York: Coward-McCann, 1970.

Conrad, Jessie. *Joseph Conrad and His Circle.* New York: Dutton, 1935.

———. *Joseph Conrad as I Knew Him.* Garden City, N.Y.: Doubleday, Page, 1927.

Conrad, John. *Joseph Conrad: Times Remembered.* Cambridge: Cambridge University Press, 1981.

Coppola, Eleanor. *Notes.* New York: Simon and Schuster, 1979. (On *Apocalypse Now*)

Cowie, Peter. *Coppola: The Director as Visionary.* New York: Da Capo, 1994.

Denton, Clive, and Kingsley Canham. *The Hollywood Professionals.* Vol. 5: King Vicor, John Cromwell, and Mervyn Leroy. New York: Barnes, 1976.

Fleishman, Avrom. *Narrated Films: Storytelling Situations in Cinema History.* Baltimore: Johns Hopkins University Press, 1992.

Ford, Ford Madox. *Joseph Conrad: A Personal Remembrance.* Boston: Little, Brown, 1924.

Gaines, Janet, ed. *Classical Hollywood Narrative.* Durham: Duke University Press, 1992.

Giddings, Robert, Keith Selby, and Chris Wensley. *Screening the Novel: The Theory and Practice of Literary Dramatization.* New York: St. Martin's Press, 1990.

Gillon, Andrew. *Joseph Conrad: Comparative Essays.* Edited by Raymond Brebach. Lubbock, Texas: Texas Tech University Press, 1994. Contains an essay on adapting Conrad to the screen. This essay appears in a different form under the title "Adapting Conrad to Film," *The Conradian* 13, no. 2 (December, 1985), 158-70.

Goodwin, Michael, and Naomi Wise. *On the Edge: The Life and Times of Francis Coppola.* New York: Morrow, 1989.

Guerard, Albert. *Conrad the Novelist.* Cambridge: Harvard University Press, 1962.

Gurko, Leo. *Joseph Conrad: Giant in Exile.* New York: Macmillan, 1979.

Hawthorn, Jeremy. *Joseph Conrad: Narrative Techniques and Ideological Commitment.* London: Edward Arnold, 1990.

Jean-Aubry, Gerard. *The Sea Dreamer: A Biography of Joseph Conrad.* Garden City, N.Y.: Doubleday, 1957.

Kael, Pauline. *Kiss Kiss Bang Bang.* New York: Bantam Books, 1969.

Kantor, Bernard R., Irwin R. Blacker, and Anne Kramer, eds. *Directors at Work: Interviews with American Film Makers.* New York: Funk and Wagnalls, 1970.

Karl, Frederick, *A Reader's Guide to Joseph Conrad.* Revised Edition. New York: Farrar, Straus, and Giroux, 1970.

———. *Joseph Conrad: The Three Lives, A Biography.* New York: Farrar, Straus and Giroux, 1979.

Keyser, Les. *Hollywood in the Seventies.* New York: Barnes, 1981.

Klein, Michael, and Gillian Parker, eds. *The English Novel and the Movies.* New York: Ungar, 1981.

Knowles, Owen. *A Conrad Chronology.* Boston: G. K. Hall, 1990.

Koszarski, Richard, ed. *Hollywood Directors: 1941-76.* Oxford: Oxford University Press, 1977.

Krenn, Heliéna. *Conrad's Lingard Trilogy: Empire, Race, and Women in the Maylay Novels.* New York: Garland, 1990.

Land, Stephen. *Paradox and Polarity in the Fiction of Joseph Conrad.* New York: St. Martin's Press, 1984.

Landy, Marcia. *British Genres: Cinema and Society, 1930-60.* Princeton, N.J.: Princeton University Press, 1991.

La Valley, Albert J., ed. *Focus on Hitchcock.* Englewood Cliffs, N.J.: Prentice-Hall, 1972.

Lester, John. *Conrad and Religion.* New York: St. Martin's Press, 1988.

McCann, Richard Dyer, ed. *Film: A Montage of Theories.* New York: Dutton, 1966.

McDougal, Stuart Y. *Made into Movies: From Literature to Film.* New York: Holt, Rinehart, and Winston, 1985.

McGilligan, Patrick, ed. *Backstory 2: Interviews with Scriptwriters.* Berkeley: University of California Press, 1991.

Meyers, Jeffrey. *Joseph Conrad: A Biography.* New York: Scribner's, 1991.

Moss, Robert. *The Films of Carol Reed.* New York: Columbia University Press, 1987.

Murdock, Marvin, ed. *Conrad: A Collection of Critical Essays.* Englewood Cliffs, N.J.: Prentice-Hall, 1966.

Murfin, Ross C. *Lord Jim: After the Truth.* Twayne Masterworks Series. New York: Twayne, 1992.

Nadelhaft, Ruth L. *Joseph Conrad.* Atlantic Highlands, N.J.: Humanities Press International, 1991.

Newhouse, Neville H. *Joseph Conrad.* New York: Arco, 1968.

Page, Norman. *A Conrad Companion.* New York: St. Martin's Press, 1986.

Phillips, Gene D. *Major Film Directors of the American and British Cinema.* Cranbury, N.J.: Associated University Presses, 1990.

Ray, Martin. *Joseph Conrad: Interviews and Recollections.* Iowa City: University of Iowa Press, 1990.

Rising, Catharine. *Darkness at Heart: Fathers and Sons in Conrad.* New York: Greenwood Press, 1990.

Ryall, Tom. *Alfred Hitchcock and the British Cinema.* Chicago: University of Illinois Press, 1986.

Sherry, Norman. *Conrad.* New York: Thames and Hudson, 1988. (An abridgement of Sherry's two biographies of Conrad.)

Smith, David R., ed. *Joseph Conrad's Under Western Eyes: Beginnings, Revisions, Final Forms: Five Essays.* Hamden, Conn.: Arcon, 1991.

Spoto, Donald. *The Art of Alfred Hitchcock: Fifty Years of His Motion Pictures.* Second edition. New York: Anchor Books, 1992.

Tennant, Roger. *Joseph Conrad.* New York: Atheneum, 1981.

Thomas, Charles Samuel. *Encountering Directors.* New York: Capricorn, 1972.

Thomas, Nicholas, ed. *The International Dictionary of Films and Filmmakers.* Revised edition. 4 vols. London: St. James Press, 1990-93.

Truffaut, Francois. *Hitchcock.* Revised Edition. New York: Simon and Schuster, 1985.

Wagner, Geoffrey. *The Novel and the Cinema.* Teaneck, N.J.: Fairleigh Dickinson University Press, 1975.

Wollaeger, Mark A. *Joseph Conrad and the Fictions of Skepticism.* Stanford: Stanford University Press, 1991.

Wapshott, Nicholas. *Carol Reed: A Biography.* New York: Knopf, 1994.

Yacowar, Maurice. *Hitchcock's British Movies.* Hamden, Conn.: Archon Books, 1977.

B. Articles

Alpert, Hollis. "A Director Redeems Himself." *Saturday Review,* March 6, 1965, p. 39.

Anderegg, Michael A. "Conrad and Hitchcock: *The Secret Agent* Inspires *Sabotage.*" *Literature/Film Quarterly,* 3 (Summer, 1973), 215-25.

Cahir, Linda Costanzo. "Narratological Parallels in Joseph Conrad's *Heart of Darkness* and Francis Ford Coppola's *Apocalypse Now. Literature/Film Quarterly,* 20, no. 3 (1992), 181-87.

Chui, Tony. "Francis Ford Coppola's Cinematic *Apocalypse* is at Hand." *New York Times* (August 12, 1979), sec. 2:1, 17.

Cohen, Paula Marantz. "Conrad's *Secret Agent* and Hitchcock's *Sabotage.*" *Literature/Film Quarterly* 22, no. 3 (1994), 199-208.

Conradian, The. 1 (1969)–26 (1994)

Conradiana. 1 (1969)–26 (1994)

Conrad News. (Conrad Club of Poland) 1 (1981)–11 (1992).

Cordero, Caroline Kirk. "Mistah Kurtz—He Alive." *Premiere,* March, 1994, p. 97.

Davis, Roderick. "Conrad Cinematized: *The Duellists.*" *Literature/Film Quarterly* 8 (Spring, 1980), 125-32.

Ferguson, Otis T. "Methods of Madness: *Victory.*" *New Republic,* January 27, 1941, p. 104.

Greene, Graham. "The Novelist and the Cinema: A Personal Experience." In *International Film Annual,* no. 2 (New York: Doubleday, 1958), pp. 54-58.

Greiff, Louis K. "Soldier, Sailor, Surfer, Chef: Conrad's Ethics and the Margins of *Apocalypse Now.*" *Literature/Film Quarterly* 20, n. 3 (1992), 188-98.

Guarner, Jose Luis. "*The Heart of the Forest.*" *Film Gazette* 18, no. 5 (May, 1988), 8.

Hall, Mordaunt. "The Screen: *Lord Jim.*" *New York Times,* November 16, 1925, p. 19.

———. "The Screen: *The Rescue.*" *New York Times,* January 14, 1929, p. 20.

———. "The Screen: *Road to Romance.*" *New York Times,* October 10, 1927, p. 24.

Joseph Conrad Today. 1 (1976)–19 (1994).

Katkutani, Michiko, "Books into Movies." *New York Times Book Review,* January 10, 1983, p. 39.

Kirschner, Paul. "Conrad and the Film." *The Quarterly of Radio, TV, and Film.* [now *Film Quarterly*] 11, no. 9 (Summer, 1957), 343-53.

Kennedy, Harlan. "*Nostromo.*" *American Film* 15, no. 6 (March 1990), 27-31, 53-55.

Klein, Michael and Gillian Parker, eds. *The English Novel and the Movies.* New York: Ungar, 1981.

"*Laughing Anne.*" *New York Times.* April 8, 1954, p. 15.

Myers, Jeffrey. *Joseph Conrad.* New York: Scribner's, 1991.

Nugent, Frank. "The Screen: *Razumov.*" *New York Times,* March 9, 1937, p. 27.

Riley, Brooks. "*Heart* Transplant." *Film Comment,* 15, no. 1 (September-October, 1979), 26-27.

Suid, Lawrence. "Hollywood and Vietnam." *Film Comment,* 15, no. 1 (September-October, 1979), 20-25.

Thomaier, William. "Conrad on the Screen." *Films in Review,* 16, no. 10 (December, 1970), 611-20.

Thompson, Richard. "John Milius Interviewed." *Film Comment* 12, no. 4 (July-August, 1976), 10-21. (Contains extracts from the first draft of the scenario for *Apocalypse Now.*)

"A Tourneur Work: *Victory.*" *New York Times,* December 18, 1919, p. 4.

Tucker, Ken. "*Heart of Darkness* on Cable." *Entertainment Weekly,* March 11, 1994, p. 40.

Updike, John. "Seen the Film? Read the Book!" *New York Times.* June 28, 1987, sec. 2:1, 28.

Variety: Film Reviews, 1907-80. 13 vols. New York: Garland, 1983.

Vermilyea, Jerry. "Margaret Lockwood: Part II." *Films in Review* 42, nos. 3-4 (March-April, 1991), 88.

Vineberg, Steve. "The Routes into Conrad on Filming: *Under Western Eyes* and *Outcast of the Islands.*" *Literature/Film Quarterly* 15, no. 1 (Winter, 1987), 22-27.

Wald, Jerry. "Screen Adaptation." *Films in Review* 5, no. 1 (February, 1954), 62-67.

Watson, Wallace. "Conrad and Film." *Conradiana* 11, no. 3 (1979), 209-27.

C. Unpublished Materials

Conrad, Joseph. Unpublished Letter from Joseph Conrad to J. B. Pinker, June 17, 1919, advising his agent of the sale of the American screen rights to his fiction.

Frost, Frank. "The Films of Richard Books." Unpublished Ph.D. Dissertation. Los Angeles: University of Southern California, 1976.

Houze, William C. "Philosophy, Politics, and Morality in *The Secret Agent* as a Novel and Play: A Comparative Study." Unpublished Ph.D. Dissertation. Syracuse, N.Y.: Syracuse University, 1980. An abridged version of this dissertation appears under the title "*The Secret Agent* from Novel to Play: The Implications of Conrad's Handling of Structure," *Conradiana*, 13, no. 2 (Summer, 1981), 109-27.

Filmography

(Note: Films about which the author could find no further information, such as the 1987 German version of *Victory*, have not been listed below.)

Victory (Paramount-Artcraft, 1919)
Director: Maurice Tourneur
Screenplay: Stephen Fox (pseudonym of Jules Furthman), based on the novel
Cinematography: Rene Guissart
Cast: Jack Holt (Axel Heyst), Seena Owen (Alma), Lon Chaney (Ricardo), Wallace Beery (Schomberg), Ben Deely (Mr. Jones), Laura Winston (Mrs. Schomberg), Bull Montana (Pedro), George Nicholis (Davidson).

Lord Jim (Famous-Players-Paramount, 1925), 67 min.
Director: Victor Fleming
Screenplay: John Russell, based on the novel
Cast: Percy Maremount (Lord Jim), Shirley Mason (Jewel), Noah Beery (Captain Brown), Raymond Hatton (Cornelius), Joseph Dowling (Stein), George Magrill (Dain Waris).

The Silver Treasure (Fox 1926)
Director: Rowland V. Lee
Screenplay: Robert N. Lee, based on *Nostromo*
Cast: George O'Brien (Nostromo), Joan Renee (Giselle), Lou Tellegen (Stoillo), Helen D'Algy (Linda), Daniel Markarenko (Giorgio), Evelyn Selbie (Teresa), Stewart Rome (Gould), Hedda Hopper (Mrs. Gould), Otto Matieson (Decoud).

The Road to Romance (MGM, 1927), 60 minutes
Director: John S. Robertson
Screenplay: Josephine Lovett, based on *Romance*
Cast: Ramon Novarro (Don Jose), Marceling Day (Serafina), Marc McDermott (Populo), Roy D'Arcy (Don Balthazar), Otto Matieson (Don Carlos), Cesare Gravina (Juan Castro).

The Rescue (United Artists, 1929)
Director: Herbert Brenon
Producer: Samuel Goldwyn
Screenplay: Elizabeth Meehan, based on the novel
Cinematography: George Barnes
Music: Hugo Riesenfeld
Production Design: William Cameron Menzies
Editors: Katherine Hilliker and H. H. Caldwell
Cast: Ronald Colman (Tom Lingard), Lily Damita (Lady Edith Travers), Alfred Hickman (Mr. Travers), Theodore von Eltz (Carter), John Davidson (Hassim), Philip Strange (D'Alacere), Bernard Siegel (Jorgensen), Soljin (Daman), Louis Morrison (Shaw), Duke Kahanamoki (Jaffir), George Regas (Wasub).

Dangerous Paradise (Paramount-Famous Players, 1930, 60 minutes)
Director: William A. Wellman
Producer: Adolph Zukor and Jesse L. Lasky
Screenplay: William Slavens McNutt and Grover Jones, based on *Victory*
Cinematography: Archie J. Stout
Music: Leo Robin and Richard Whiting
Production Design: Joseph Youngerman
Cast: Nancy Carroll (Alma), Richard Arlen (Heyst), Warner Oland (Schomberg), Gustav von Seyffertitz (Mr. Jones), Francis McDonald (Ricardo), George Kotsonaros (Pedro), Dorothea Wolberg (Mrs. Schomberg), Clarence H. Wilson (Zangiacomo), Evelyn Selbie (his wife), Willie Fung (Wang), Wong Wing (his wife).

Razumov (Garrison Films, 1936), 97 minutes
Director: Marc Allégret
Producer: André Daven
Screenplay: H. Wilhelm, L. Lustig, and Jacques
Viot, based on *Under Western Eyes*
Cinematography: Michel Kelber
Cast: Pierre Fresnay (Razumov), Jean-Louis
Barrault (Haldin), Michel Simon (Lespara), Danielle Parola
(Nathalie), Jacques Copeau (Mikulin), Pierre Renoir (Mikulin's
Agent), Gabrio (Nikita).

Sabotage (Gaumont-British, 1936), 76 minutes
Director: Alfred Hitchcock
Producer: Michael Balcon and Ivor Montagu
Screenplay: Charles Bennett, Alma Reville, Ian
Hay, Helen Simpson, E. V. H.
Emmett, based on *The Secret Agent*
Cinematography: Bernard Knowles
Music: Louis Levy
Production Design: Otto Werndorff and Albert Jullion
Editor: Charles Frend
Cast: Sylvia Sidney (Mrs. Verloc), Oscar
Homolka (Verloc), John Loder (Ted), Desmond Tester (Stevie),
William Dewhurst (Mr. Chatman, the Professor), Martita Hunt
(his daughter). The film was initially released as *A Woman Alone*
in the USA.

Victory (Paramount, 1940, 77 minutes)
Director: John Cromwell
Producer: Anthony Veiller
Screenplay: John L. Balderston, based on the
novel
Cinematography: Leo Tover
Editor: William Shea
Cast: Fredric March (Heyst), Betty Field
(Alma), Sir Cedric Hardwicke (Mr. Jones), Sig Rumann
(Schomberg), Margaret Wycherly (Mrs. Schomberg), Jerome
Cowan (Ricardo), Fritz Feld (Signor Makanoff), Rafaela Ottiano

(Madame Makanoff), Lionel Royce (Pedro), Chester Gan (Wang).

An Outcast of the Islands (London Films, 1952), 102 minutes
Director: Carol Reed
Producer: Carol Reed
Screenplay: William Fairchild, based on the novel
Cinematography: John Wilcox
Music: Brian Easdale
Production Design: Vincent Korda
Editor: Bert Bates
Cast: Trevor Howard (Willems), Ralph Richardson (Captain Tom Lingard), Robert Morley (Almayer), Wendy Hiller (Mrs. Almayer), Kerma (Aïssa), George Coulouris (Balalatchi), A. D. Bramble (Badavi), Winfred Hyde-Whyte (Vinck), Annabel Morley (Nina Almayer). Running time in USA is 93 minutes.

Face to Face: The *Secret Sharer* segment (RKO, 1952), 90 minutes (total running time)
Director: John Brahm
Producer: Huntington Hartford
Screenplay: Aeneas MacKenzie, based on the short story
Cinematography: Karl Struss
Music: Hugo Friedhofer
Production Design: Edward Ilous
Editor: Otto Meyer
Cast: James Mason (The Captain), Michael Pate (Leggatt), Gene Lockhart (Captain Archibald), Albert Sharpe (First Mate), Sean McClory (Second Mate), Alec Harfor (Ship's Cook).

Laughing Anne (Republic, 1954), 90 minutes
Director: Herbert Wilcox
Producer: Herbert Wilcox
Screenplay: Pamela Bower, based on "Because of the Dollars"

Cinematography: Max Greene (color)
Music: Anthony Collins
Editor: Basil Warren
Cast: Wendell Corey (Captain Davidson), Margaret Lockwood (Laughing Anne), Forrest Tucker (Jem Farrell), Robert Harris (Joseph Conrad), Ronald Shiner (Nobby Clark), Susan Davidson (Helen Shingler), Sean Lynch (David).

Lord Jim (Columbia Pictures, 1965), 154 minutes
Director: Richard Brooks
Producer: Richard Brooks
Screenplay: Richard Brooks, based on the novel
Cinematography: Frederick Young (color)
Music: Bronislau Kaper
Production Design: Bill Hutchinson and Earnest Archer
Editor: Alan Osbiston
Cast: Peter O'Toole (Lord Jim), James Mason (Gentleman Brown), Curt Jurgens (Cornelius), Eli Wallach (The General), Jack Hawkins (Marlow), Paul Lukas (Stein), Akim Tamiroff (Schomberg), Daliah Lavi (The Girl), Ichizo Itami (Dain Waris), Tatsuo Saito (Chief Doramin), Eric Young (Malay), Andrew Keir (Brierly).

The Secret Sharer (Encyclopedia Britannica Films, 1973), 30 minutes
Director: Larry Yust
Producer: Larry Yust, Nina Kleinberg
Screenplay: Larry Yust, based on the short story
Cinematography: Isadore Mankovsky (color)
Cast: David Soul (The Captain), Aaron Kincaid (Leggatt), Paul Brinegar (Captain Archbold), William Benedict (Chief Mate), Patrick Campbell (Steward).

The Rover (Selmur Productions, 1967), 103 minutes
Director: Terrence Young
Producer: Alfredo Bini
Screenplay: Lucian Vincenzoni and Jo Eisinger, based on the novel
Cinematography: Leonida Barboni (color)

Music: Ennio Morricone
Production Design: Gianni Polidori
Editor: Peter Thornton
Cast: Anthony Quinn (Peyroll), Rita Hayworth (Caterina), Anna Schiaffino (Arlette), Richard Johnson (Lieutenant Réal), Ivo Garrani (Scevola), Mino Doro (Dussard), Luciano Rossi (Michel), Mirko Valentin (Jacot), Anthony Dawson (Captain Vincent).

The Duellists (Enigma Productions, 1977), 95 minutes
Director: Ridley Scott
Screenplay: Gerald Vaughan-Hughes, based on "The Duel"
Cinematography: Frank Tidy (color)
Production Design: Bryan Graves
Editor: Pamela Power
Cast: Keith Carradine (D'Hubert), Harvey Keitel (Feraud), Cristina Raines (Adele), Edward Fox (Colonel), Robert Stephens (Treillard), John McEnery (Commander), Albert Finney (Fouche).

Apocalypse Now (Zoetrope Studios, 1979), 153 minutes
Director: Francis Ford Coppola
Producers: Fred Roos, Gray Frederickson
Screenplay: Francis Ford Coppola, John Milius, Michael Herr, based on "Heart of Darkness"
Cinematography: Vittorio Storaro (color)
Music: Carmine Coppola, Francis Ford Coppola
Production Design: Dean Tavoularis
Editors: Walter Murch, Gerald B. Greenberg, Lisa Fruchtman
Cast: Martin Sheen (Captain Benjamin Willard), Marlon Brando (Colonel Walter E. Kurtz), Robert Duvall (Lieutenant Colonel Bill Kilgore), Frederic Forrest (Chef), Dennis Hopper (Photojournalist), G. D. Spradlin (General Cameron), Harrison Ford (Colonel Lucas), Sam Bottoms (Lance B. Johnson).

Heart of the Forest (Arandano S. A., 1979), 105 minutes

Director: Manuel Gutiérrez Aragon
Screenplay: Luís Magino, based on "Heart of
        Darkness"
Cinematography: Téo Escamilla (color)
Editor: José Salcedo
Cast: Norman Briski (Juan), Angela Molina
(Amparo), Luixxs Politti (Andarin), Victor Valverde (Suso), Santiago Ramos (Atilano).

Heart of Darkness (TNT-TV, first telecast March 13, 1994), 105 minutes

Director: Nicholas Roeg
Cast: Tim Roth (Charles Marlow), John
        Malkovich (Kurtz).

1. Alfred Hitchcock directing Oscar Homolka in *Sabotage*, based on Joseph Conrad's *The Secret Agent*. (Museum of Modern Art/Still Film Archive)

2. Ramon Novarro in The *Road to Romance*, based on the novel *Romance* by Joseph Conrad and Ford Maddox Ford. (Museum of Modern Art/Still Film Archive)

3. Ronald Colman and Lily Damita in *The Rescue*. Ronald Colman plays Captain Tom Lingard, the same role played by Ralph Richardson in *An Outcast of the Islands* twenty-two years later. (Museum of Modern Art/Film Stills Archive)

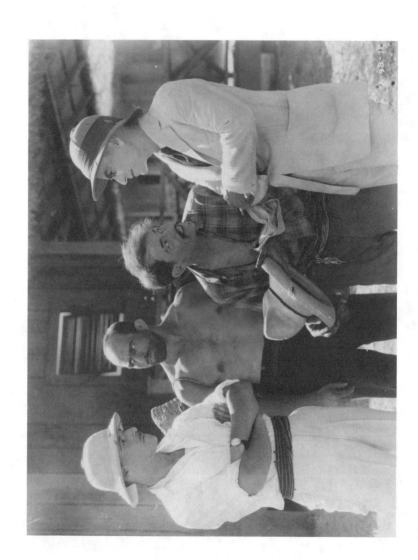

4. Jack Holt confronts Bull Montana, Lon Chaney, and Ben Deely in the first version of *Victory*. (Museum of Modern Art/Film Stills Archive)

5. Gustav von Seyffertitz (left) and Francis McDonald (right) menace Warner Oland (middle) in the second version of *Victory*, called *Dangerous Paradise*. (Museum of Modern Art/Film Stills Archive)

6. Fredric March is suspicious about Sig Rumann in the third version of *Victory*. (Museum of Modern Art/Film Stills Archive)

7. Michel Simon, the distinguished French actor in *Razumov*, the French
    film of *Under Western Eyes*. (Museum of Modern Art/Film Stills
    Archive.

8. Sylvia Sidney and Desmond Tester examine a sailboat as the villain of *Sabotage*, based on Conrad's *Secret Agent*, eyes both of them menacingly. (Museum of Modern Art/Film Stills Archive)

9. Trevor Howard plays the title role in An *Outcast of the Islands*. (Museum of Modern Art/Film Stills Archive)

10. Tom Lingard (Ralph Richardson) confronts the title character in *An Outcast of the Islands*. Lingard was played by Ronald Colman as a younger man in *The Rescue*. (Museum of Modern Art / Film Stills Archive)

11. James Mason plays a ship captain in "The Secret Sharer," one segment of the omnibus film *Face to Face*. (Movie Star News Film Archive)

12. Wendell Corey is the hero of *Laughing Anne*, talking to Robert Harris, who plays Joseph Conrad in the film. (Collectors Book Store)

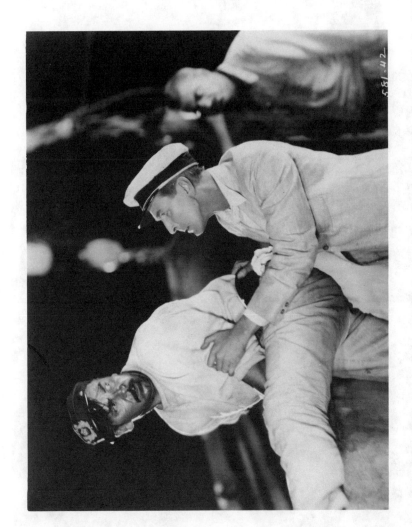

13. Lord Jim (Percy Marmount, right) tries to keep Captain Brown (Noah Beery, left) from jumping ship in the first version of *Lord Jim*. (Museum of Modern Art/Film Stills Archive)

14. Peter O'Toole in the title role of the second version of *Lord Jim*. (Museum of Modern Art Film Stills Archive)

15. Anthony Quinn is a pirate in *The Rover*. (Museum of Modern Art/Film Stills Archive)

16.   Keith Carradine (left, top) and Harvey Keitel play *The Duellists* in the
film of *The Duel*. (Museum of Modern Art/Film Stills Archive)

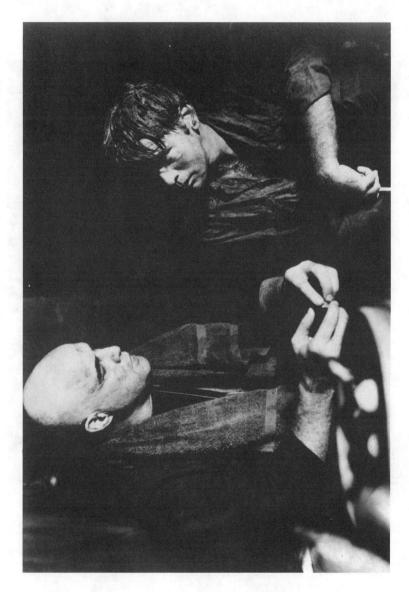

17. Col. Kurtz (Marlon Brando) harrangues Captain Ben Willard (Martin Sheen) in *Apocalypse Now*, based on *Heart of Darkness*.

18. Captain Ben Willard is captured by natives in *Apocalypse Now*, based on *Heart of Darkness*. (Museum of Modern Art/Film Stills Archive)

19. Joseph Conrad in later years. (The Harry Ransom Humanities Research Center, the University of Texas at Austin)

Index

ARS INTERPRETANDI
THE ART OF INTERPRETATION

The title indicates the open-ended nature of this series. It includes books and monographs in all literatures and has as its primary focus the hermeneutic act. Topics are not restricted to critical theory but can range from studies on a landmark poem or poetic cycle to broader essays on a literary generation or a genre, etc., provided they make clear the extent to which they insert themselves into the past or contemporary critical and self-critical discourse. Prospective authors are invited to send their proposal or an outline and text sample to the editor of the series prior to submitting a manuscript. The publisher requires a camera-ready copy of a minimum length of 200 pages and a maximum length of 400 pages.

For information write to: Raymond Gay-Crosier, Department of Romance Languages and Literatures, University of Florida, Gainesville, Florida, 32611, USA or call (904) 392-2017 or 2018.